BAGS WITH PAPER AND STITCH

BAGS WITH PAPER AND STITCH

Isobel Hall

INTERWEAVE PRESS
interweave.com

Acknowledgments

Writing this book has given me enormous pleasure and without the help, support, and photography from my husband, Eric, it would not have been possible. My thanks go to him first and foremost.

The value of the positive, constructive advice and encouragement from my daughters, Kerri and Xantha, is incalculable and I feel most fortunate to have had their unstinting support.

I would also like to thank all of my friends and in particular Yvonne Catlender and Les Rylett for their generous donations, enthusiasm, and time.

This book is dedicated to my mother who started it all in my formative years.

First published in the United States by
Interweave Press LLC
201 East Fourth Street
Loveland, CO 80537-4632
Interweave.com

Library of Congress Cataloging-in-Publication Data

Hall, Isobel.
    Bags with paper and stitch : innovative surface techniques for embellished bags / Isobel Hall, author.
            p. cm.
    Includes bibliographical references and index.
    ISBN 978-1-59668-051-7 (pbk.)
    1. Handbags. 2. Sewing. 3. Fancy work. I. Title.
    TT667.H32 2007
    646.4'8--dc22
2007008977

10 9 8 7 6 5 4 3 2 1

Reproduction by Spectrum Colour Ltd. Ipswich
Printed by Craft Print International Ltd. Singapore
Photography by Michael Wicks except pages 44, 45, 53, 54, 55, 56, 59, 60, 79, 84, 117 (top) and 122

Page one: Evening bag made from bookbinder's tissue. Pattern added with encaustic wax over an embossing tray. Colored with Twinkling H_2O paints.

Page two: Leather-effect bag made from reconstituted silk paper which was bonded to Softsculpt.

Page three: Hand-woven bag representing a ploughed field. Embroidered on abaca paper in Sorbello stitch.

Opposite: Bag made from cocoon-stripping paper with impressed paper clay decoration.

Contents

INTRODUCTION

I am often asked, "But what do you do with the paper you make on the workshops you run?" Putting it into sketchbooks or making pictures for the wall doesn't necessarily fulfill a need. I had to find a good reason to work with it. I spent a couple of years making books and filling them with ideas and postcard collections, and then, quite by chance, I was asked to make a bag and Bingo! that was that. From that day forward I was hooked. I had found the right thing to do. For centuries embroiderers have been working at their craft producing decorative but useful things. I have always wanted to produce items I have made from scratch and that are useful but also involve modern techniques. I was home at last. I was catapulted into making bags from paper. Making paper and making bags go hand in hand.

This is therefore a book for beginners in the art of papermaking as well as a beginner's guide on how to utilize the paper that is all around us. Many of the bags in this book are really special-occasion bags as they take a long time to embroider. They are intended to be exclusive, and they have all been "road tested" to ensure suitability. I use the bags I make, and I'm not known locally as "the bag lady" for nothing!

Some bags are more robust than others, and I do take care of my bags. There is a superstition in Spain that if you put your bag on the floor, your money will run out. Spanish ladies carry little hooks that attach their bags to restaurant tabletops when they go out. I don't go that far, but bags made from paper should be looked after. However, if you want your bag to be really robust, then working with fibers bonded with acrylic gloss medium is your best option.

Obtaining the correct backing for the bag is also important. I have experimented with various backings, and my favorite is batting made from natural fibers. Batting made from man-made fibers is cheaper, but it tends to be thicker and not quite so pliable. Curtain interlining is a good substitute, but it does fray. This only matters if the seams in the bag show. Sometimes colored felt can be a good option.

I like to pay particular attention to the lining. A lovely, satin lining feels sumptuous, and it can bring a bag to life. Suede polyester looks good and dyes well. Look for bargains on the remnant counters as this keeps the cost of the bag down. Leather pieces can also be bought quite cheaply from specialist suppliers.

I like to work areas of interest onto both sides of the bag. It takes more time, but it is well worth the effort. If you only work on one side, the results can look a bit mean.

This book is intended to be used as a starting point and as a guide to experimentation. Using new materials and experimenting with new techniques can be both exciting and rewarding. The resulting papers do not have to be made into bags, and I hope that by experimentation you will find lots of uses for the techniques in this book, as many of them can also be applied to working with fabrics.

Have fun but note that if you are working with potentially hazardous materials, you really should work in a well-ventilated area and wear a respirator and mask.

Bag made from textured cotton rag paper colored with fabric paints and alcohol inks, Glitterati fusible film, and wire mesh, appliquéd in places and protected by Sorbello stitch.

Handles

Handles can make or break a bag, and it's great fun to experiment with different and sometimes amusing ones. I'm always on the lookout for great handles to personalize my bags, and it's even better if they feel comfortable in the hand.

Cord handles

Wool, silk, or cotton cords can be plaited, wrapped, beaded, and mixed with other fibers. Plastic or leather piping, sold for jewelery making, can look very effective, as can shoelaces. Try plaiting leather strips and adding homemade beads made from polymer clay or use heavy rope bought from hardware stores. Cord can also be wrapped with bobbly yarn for a textured effect.

Cane handles

Cane handles can be bought quite cheaply from craft stores and look very professional. They can be bound with wool or thread to make them look more interesting.

Plastic handles

Plastic carrier bags are a good source of cheap, readily available handles. They go well with little chunky bags. When they are wrapped they look very different (see bag opposite).

Clear plastic tubing

The clear tubing sometimes used by winemakers for siphoning homemade wine can be used to make handles, though these sometimes need embellishment to stop them looking too cheap: try decorating the ends with silk pods or binding them with thread or ribbon. Remember that you have to be able to get the needle through the tubing, so don't buy it too thick (or try pulling the needle through with a pair of pliers).

You could try wrapping the tubing with strips of silk paper and then wrap evenly spaced thread first in one direction and then the other. I use double-sided tape to anchor the ribbons, strips, or threads. Keep a wipe handy for the needle as it will get sticky when you sew the tubing to the bag.

Reused handles

Look in flea markets or thrift shops for vintage frame purses and clasp bags. The handles can be removed and reused for your creations.

Paper handles

The handles on brown paper shopping bags are cheap and extremely useful. They may look unappealing at first, but when they are wrapped they can look very different. Try wrapping them with wool, thick and thin yarns, cord, strips of silk paper, and lengths of fabric. Some bags look best if the paper handle is wrapped with matching machine embroidery thread. This is time consuming but it is well worth the effort.

Store-bought paper embellished with merino tops, machine and handstitching. The plastic shopping bag handles were wrapped to disguise their origin.

Wrapped compressed paper

Wrapped compressed paper can make good long shoulder straps. Finding the right material to wrap it with is the key to this technique.

Curtain weights

Look for fabric linked lengths of weights sold in curtain shops to make net curtains hang straight. They color well and can make good cheap shoulder bag straps (see page 119).

Dress belts

Dress belts can sometimes fit the shape of your bag. They usually need to be dyed to tone with the bag. A quick-and-easy method is to cut the ends off and then rub alcohol inks on both sides. I have found that it is best to lay the belt flat on a covered, protected surface and do one side at a time. I use batting strips to apply the inks, which dry very quickly. Keep the used batting as the ink on the batting pad can be reactivated with blending fluid at a later date. (Test the cut-off pieces of the belt first for waterproofing. Sometimes a little color can rub off when it is wet.) Polishing with leather polish can help to waterproof it.

Tubular knitting wire

Knitted wire tubing can be stitched into and because it is pliable it can be manipulated. It is therefore suitable for use as bag decoration and for handles (see page 80).

Natural handles

Sticks you have found can make unusual but effective handles. Look for straight sticks, but make sure that they retain some character. It is well worth taking the time to sand any sticks you find, as this makes them easier to handle—you don't want splinters in your hand when you go out with your bag. Sticks can be colored with fiber-reactive dye when they have been sanded.

Bought handles

Bought handles can sometimes fit in with your bag better if they are first wrapped with matching yarn. It may even suit the bag better if the handles are painted or enameled (see page 32).

Plaited rope

Plaited rope can make good straps for shoulder bags. For added interest and texture, tie a large knot in the ends, fray the cords, and tease them until they are fluffy.

Wrapped ring handles

Rings sold for bag handles sometimes look nice as they are, but often they do not suit the character of your bag. They could be painted, enameled, or simply wrapped with a matching thread or ribbon to overcome this problem (see page 100).

Handwoven iridescent film with strips of silk paper woven through. This bag features plastic wrapped handles with silk cocoons to disguise the ends.

Black plastic ribbed cable protector

Black plastic ribbed cable protector is worth tracking down to make unusual handles. The plastic should not be too rigid or brittle, as it can snap easily. Unfortunately this is not a good quality for bag handles! Pulling the needle through with a pair of pliers is often necessary when attaching the tubing to the bag.

Converting unusual materials

Look for unusual items that can be converted into handles. Handles can come in all sorts of shapes and guises.

- Sometimes necklaces are appropriate.
- Chain belts found in thrift shops can make good handles for shoulder bags.
- Plumbers' suppliers can yield some interesting options. Silver- or gold-colored ball chain links attached to sink plugs can sometimes be used on dainty little bags when the plug has been removed. I have also used flexible metal tubing sold for hot-and-cold water connections. These are sturdy and require strong, durable fabric for the bag. You need to take the strength of the fabric into consideration when designing bags using such handles.
- If you can find leather bootlaces, these are excellent for use with large wooden beads. Thread the beads on and attach the handles to the bag. They will be strong, sturdy, and will remain upright.

Fastenings

In this book I have included a variety of easily available fastenings. Zippers are an obvious choice, but suitable zippers are not easy to find. Dress zippers are difficult to use unless you devise a way to increase the size of the pulling tab. Velcro and hooked fastenings are other obvious choices. Velcro can be bought cheaply, and it can be obtained in a variety of colors. Finding magnetic fasteners used to be a problem, but they are easily available now from speciality stores.

Jewelry

Heavy medallion necklaces are fashionable at the moment. The weight of a medallion can be used to hold a flap down. Large buckles and disks on belts are also fashionable, and because they are heavy they can serve to hold a bag flap down.

Fasteners and eyelets

Fasteners and eyelets hammered in position with an eyelet tool require careful consideration. These work well with strengthened papers as paper doesn't fray, but care must be taken to ensure that the fabric is not too thick for the fastener to go through. Remember that the paper will have been bonded to batting, so it will be quite thick.

Bag made from textured paper with embossing enamels.

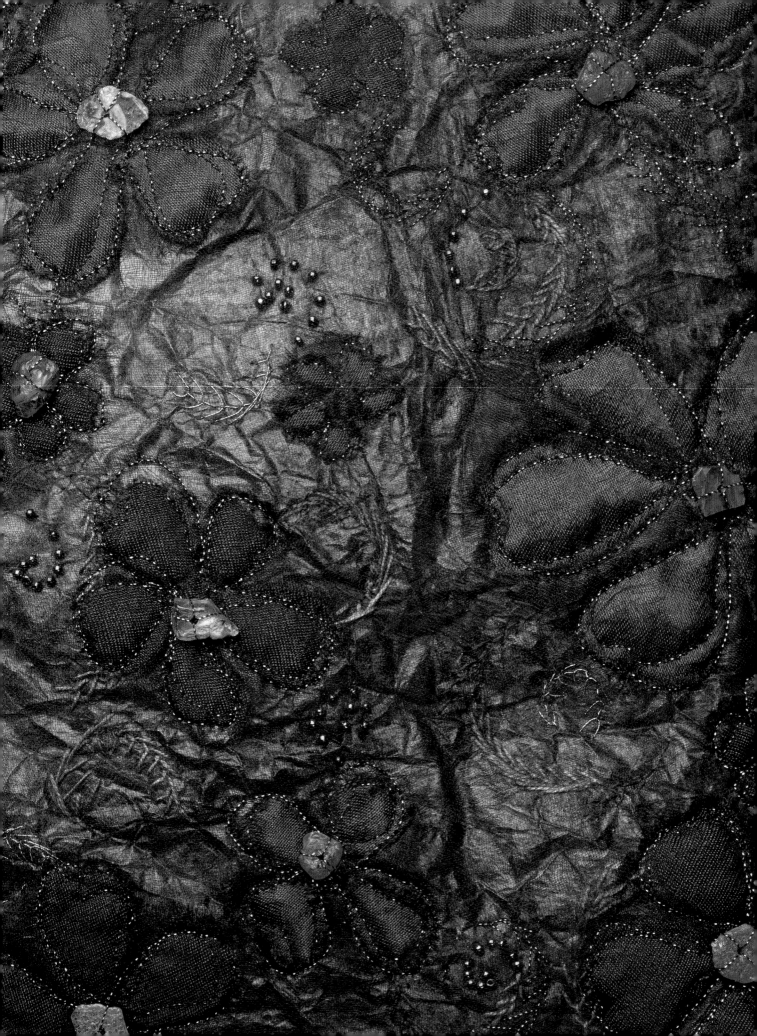

Hardware

Searching through trays of odds and ends in hardware stores can prove to be very fruitful. Door catches come in interesting shapes and sizes, as do brackets and hinges. Look for interesting shapes. The holes intended to hold screws can be used to anchor the bracket to the bag with stitches.

Buttons

Large buttons, bought or made, sewn in the center of a bag, can act as an anchor. Cord or looped ribbon, sewn on the bag flap, can then be wrapped round the button to close the bag.

Buckles and straps

If you are using buckles and straps to fasten the bag, the fabric needs to be robust enough to eliminate the possibility of tearing the holes in the strap. Use silk papers only. Even then the paper for the strap needs to be reinforced with PVA glue (polyvinyl acetate, common white glue, or carpenter's glue).

Cords and washers

The square-shaped bags in this book are fastened by tying cords that are threaded through washers. The washers need to coordinate with the bag and they can be painted, wrapped or embroidered in buttonhole stitch (see pages 103—104).

Curtain rings

Wooden curtain hoops come in varying sizes. If they are wrapped with the appropriate material, they can be used as decoration and as a means of closing the bag. The bag on page 13 uses a curtain ring, which is wrapped with ribbon. The ring was attached to the top center on one side of the bag. A large loop of fabric was sewn on the other side of the bag. To close the bag, this loop is threaded through the ring.

Encaustic wax and appliquéd flowers (see page 84 for more information on encaustic wax).

1 TAGS FOR BAGS

Personalizing bags can be really good fun. Tags, badges, brooches, trinkets, and charms can all make a contribution to the character of the bag. Attach them with split rings or little metal chains with connectors. If you are using metal rings as links, they should be attached to the bag handles prior to stitching the handles in position as they can be pulled out of the way when the handle is stitched in place. Most of the tags benefit by being backed onto another fabric, such as silk paper or pieces of leather and suede.

Embossing Enamels

YOU WILL NEED:
- 3 different colored embossing enamels
- 3 clean plastic tubs
- ink pad (or heat-fixable paint)
- heat tool
- base fabric you are embossing
- rubber stamp
- talcum powder

Opalettes embossing enamels are particularly exciting to use. They come in boxes of five colors, and the end result really looks like enamel, but it has the advantage that it can be stitched into. The basic principle is that colors need to be layered on to either embossing ink or heat-fixable paint, and then heated with a heat tool.

Method

1   Have all your materials assembled so you can carry out each stage speedily. Open the enamels you require and place each one in an empty, clean plastic tub (such as ice-cream containers) in order to keep them separate.
2   Dust the rubber stamp with talcum powder.
3   Ink up the surface you are working on. A gold ink pad invariably works well. (Another option is to use heat-fixable paint.)
4   Hold the item to be enameled over the first tub and sprinkle the powder liberally over the metal. Any excess will fall into the tub, which will make it easy for you to pour it back into the jar when you have finished.
5   Before you heat the enamel decide which color you are going to use next.
6   Heat the enamel. Remember that embossing enamels get very hot so be careful not to touch them until they are cool.
7   Sprinkle on the second layer of powder.
8   Heat and repeat—three colors usually work best.

From left to right: Embossing enamels on silk paper (A and B), metal (C), card (D) and tea bag paper (E).

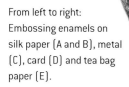

Tags Made on Silk Paper

Use silk paper scraps for these tags. This will make them robust. Any unwanted color and pattern can be obliterated with white gesso. Texture can be added with the addition of gold metal flakes or Stewart Gill Byzantia metal flakes or fresco flakes (see G, below). Applying a coat of acrylic wax over the final color is always a good idea. If you are going to stitch into the tags, they will probably need to be backed onto another sheet of silk paper or onto another fabric so that both sides look appealing.

Thin silk paper and sheers
Variation and depth of color can be added to silk paper by backing it onto a colored sheer fabric. Try stamping, embroidering, and beading strips of silk paper pieces for this technique. Remember that as these tags will not be backed onto another fabric, any stitching or beading needs to be appealing on both sides (see J, below).

Image Maker
Images can be transferred to white silk paper. If the paper is not white, it should be painted first with white gesso. When it is dry, spread Image Maker gel liberally over the front of an inkjet printed image (or color photocopy). Place the image face down on the silk paper and leave it to dry. Rub the back of the paper off with a wet paper towel. Cut the image out and bond it to a prepared surface. (Try bonding images to canvas metal-rimmed tags, see page 111.)

Stumpwork, crewelwork, and canvaswork tags
Your silk paper needs to be robust if crewelwork, stumpwork, or canvaswork is going to be embroidered as a stand-alone piece (for stumpwork on textured silk, see page 76).

Canvaswork stitches can be made on silk paper with an evenweave fabric behind. Remove the threads with tweezers when the embroidery is complete. The Christmas tree tag (see H, below) was backed onto a metal-rimmed tag. The creature on the pom-pom tag (see I, below) was worked on silk paper and backed onto leather.

An assortment of tags made from silk paper.

G

H

I

J

Embossed Metals

Embossed copper shim needs to be well anchored to the base fabric if it is to be used for bag decoration. If the edges are exposed, they can easily get bent and the metal could tear. Copper and aluminum shim is easy to cut and stitch into. Heavier metal needs careful consideration as you don't want any sharp edges that could cut you or catch on clothing when the bag is in use.

1 Lay down a protective layer. Magazines are the best background to work on for embossing.
2 Place the copper shim or aluminum sheet on the magazine.
3 Place a prepared drawing over the shim.
4 Use masking tape to attach the drawing to the shim and the magazine.
5 Use an embossing tool, an old knitting needle, or a worn-out biro to go round the outline of the design.
6 Remove the masking tape and the drawing.
7 Turn the metal over and use the embossing tools to emphasize the details.
8 Cut out the design out.
9 Color the metal with black acrylic paint, Stewart Gill Glitterati fusible film (see A and B, below) or alcohol inks (see C, D and E, below).
10 The shape can be stitched into and beaded if required.

Glitterati fusible film

This fusible film can be used over embossed metals to transfer designs or to color the metal. It works best on embossed aluminum. Place the film over the aluminum and cover it with baking parchment to protect your iron. Iron over the parchment to fuse the film to the metal. Keep looking to see if the image has transferred. When it is cool, peel it carefully off the metal. If you overheat the film it will be permanently fused

From left to right: Tags covered with Glitterati fusible film (A and B) and colored with inks (C, D and E).

Mylar Shimmer Sheetz

Mylar Shimmer Sheetz look like thin sheets of rigid plastic. When they are heated they become moldable. They come in a variety of colors and the colors can be easily altered with the use of alcohol inks. They make good tags and decorative items for bags as they are durable and can be stitched into and beaded. Any holes made by a needle will show, so some thought is needed before you stitch. As the stitches lie on the top it is best to keep them simple and to a minimum.

TIP: To begin stitching, put a knot in the end of the thread. Secure it to the back with masking tape. This prevents the thread slipping through the hole made by the needle.

Method

1 Place the Mylar on a spongy mouse pad.
2 Heat with a heat tool.
3 Press a wooden stamp into the heated Mylar.
4 Use alcohol inks to alter the color of the Mylar if necessary. (Do not use blending fluid as it will take the entire color out of the Mylar.)

Look out for unusual items with raised detail to use with Mylar. Either side of the impressed Mylar can be used. For unusual zip pulls or tags, try inserting impressed Mylar into key-ring tags, or sewing it onto metal-rimmed luggage labels.

From left to right: Two pieces of impressed Mylar placed back to back (F), impressed Mylar on leather (G), and impressed Mylar on silk paper (H and I).

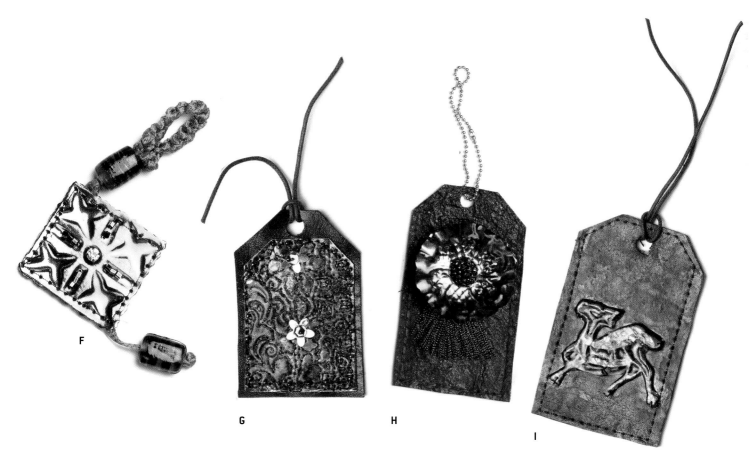

F

G

H

I

Distressed Luggage Labels

The bought card luggage label (see C, below) was distressed with tea-dye distress ink. Distress inks can be bought in a range of colors. To make this tag, a bought card label was crumpled up. (If you are going to stitch into the card and back it onto another fabric, then only one side needs to be distressed and stamped.) Distress ink was rubbed over it on one side. Water was sprayed liberally over it. It was placed between two sheets of baking parchment and ironed flat. A bought stamp was inked up and pressed onto the card, which was then embroidered. The tag was backed onto a piece of brown suede.

Computer Linen Paper

From left to right: Computer linen paper on silk paper; distressed computer printed image; distressed luggage label using tea-dye ink.

There are lots of materials available for stampers and scrapbook makers, which can be interesting for embroiderers. One such product is a paper that has fine linen bonded to it: Images can be printed on it using an ink-jet printer. It is sticky backed and once the backing is peeled off the edges can be frayed, and the image can be bonded to silk paper and stitched into. (Keep a wipe handy to clean the needle, which will get sticky.) This linen is also suitable for stamping (see page 125, Sir Lancelot tag).

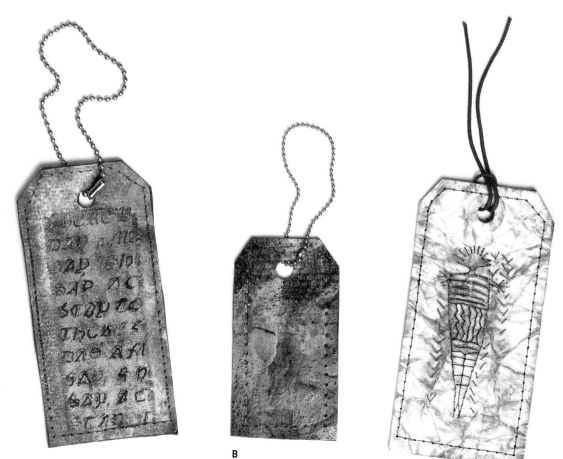

A   B   C

Computer Printed Tags

Use a photograph of a landscape or in this instance a photograph of an embroidered garden (see B, opposite. Print the image on card-stock and then distress the card-stock by painting liquid coffee over it. When this is dry, paint two layers of varnish over it and allow some of the varnish to puddle. Place two pieces of card treated in this way back to back and bond them with PVA glue.

Air-drying and Paper Clay

Working with air-drying clay has its limitations. If you are working with Crayola Model Magic, the piece must be backed onto a stabilizer in order to reduce the possibility of the clay crumbling. A coat of varnish is also advisable to protect it. Beads made from Model Magic should be also placed in areas where they will not get much wear and tear. The tag below (E) is made from silk paper with a Model Magic brooch sewn on the center. The piece is backed onto a strong stable fabric in order to give it added protection.

Paper clay is stronger and more durable than air-drying clay. The yellow initials tag (see F, below) had canvas trapped in the clay. The dry clay was painted, and when this was dry, it was embroidered in cross-stitch. Stitching needs to be kept to a minimum. The canvas embedded in the clay helped to stabilize the tag.

You could try stamping into rolled-out paper clay. The sailing boat tag (see D, below) was stamped into with a bought stamp that was inked up on a Stazon ink pad.

An assortment of tags made from paper clay.

D

E

F

Translucent Liquid Sculpey Tags

The instructions for working with liquid clay are at the back of the book (see page 107). Try the following ideas:

Stamping
Trap the stamped image between two layers of baked TLS. The ship's wheel (see D, below) was stamped using Stazon ink.

Appliqué
Color one layer of TLS and bake to set the color. Cut the image out and appliqué the image to fabric or silk paper (see frog tag, page 95).

Trapping gold flakes
Paint one layer of TLS on the glass and bake it. Sponge it with alcohol inks. Add gold flakes to the baked sheet on the glass. Paint a second layer of TLS over the gold flakes and the first layer. Bake it to set it (see B, below).

Silk paper trapped in TLS
Paint and bake the first layer of TLS. Place the colored silk paper on top of the baked TLS. Cover the silk paper and the first layer with TLS and bake. The silk paper will be trapped between the layers (see C, below). The blue color that you can see in this tag is silk paper.

Flowers trapped in TLS
Paint and bake one layer of TLS. Place a flower (in this case a hydrangea) on the first layer. Paint a second layer of TLS and bake. This hydrangea was cut out and appliquéd to stamped, embossed silk paper (see A, below).

Translucent Liquid Sculpey (TLS) tags.

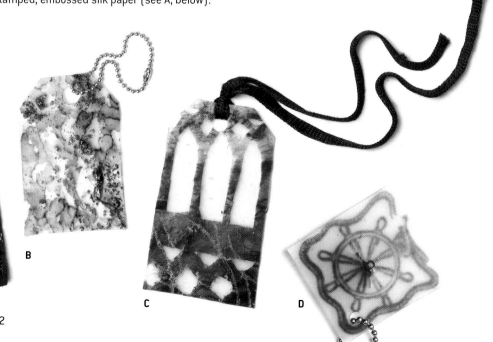

A

B

C

D

Bonded Sheers

The two tags below (C and D) were made by using a soldering iron to bond sheer fabrics on to Kunin felt. Two hearts were made for the tag in the center (C) and they were sewn to both sides of the painted canvas metal-rimmed tag.

Shrink Plastic

Shrink plastic is not one of my most favorite mediums as it is impossible to stitch into. The only way it can be stitched is if you make holes with a hole punch prior to shrinking it. It does however make durable tags. Shrink the plastic first following the manufacturer's instructions. (Don't forget to punch the hole for the metal chain to go through.) Use an ink pad to cover the plastic. Sprinkle embossing enamels over the wet ink then heat with a heat tool. Dust a stamp with talcum powder. Place the stamp on the hot enamel and leave it to cool (see A and B, below).

Angelina Fibers

The tag on the far right (see E, below) was made from an Angelina fiber patch. Angelina patches are quite robust and easy to stitch into. These patches make good tags but they are also suitable for patchwork and appliqué.

1   Use a wooden stamp.
2   Ink up the stamp on an appropriately colored ink pad.
3   Place a tuft of Angelina fibers on top of the stamp.
4   Cover the fibers with baking parchment.
5   With the iron set on low, iron the fibers until they have bonded.
6   Peel off the patch.
7   Trim the edges with scissors.

Tags A and B use shrink plastic, C and D use bonded sheers and E uses Angelica fibers.

A

B

C

D

E

The tags below were all made using a glue gun.

Glue Gun Tags and Patches

To make a patch, you will need baking parchment or a sheet of baking Teflon to work on.

1   Squeeze the required amount of glue from the gun onto the sheet. Do not touch the glue as it will be very hot.
2   Dust a rubber stamp with talcum powder and place it on the hot glue. Leave the stamp until the glue is cold and then remove it.
3   Color both sides of the glue.
4   Stitch into it and bead it.

TIPS
• Try drawing with glue on textured paper (see A, below), or squeeze glue into a bowl of cold water (see E, above left).
• The needle will get sticky when you stitch into the cold glue. It is a good idea to have a wipe handy to clean it.
• If you are dissatisfied with your first attempt at making a patch, reheat the glue with the hot gun and try again. Remember to work on baking parchment if you are reheating glue.
• Glue gun embellishments can be used to decorate bags and tags, and they are also useful to disguise the back of magnetic fasteners.

E

A

B

C

D

Embroidering with Abaca Paper

The abaca paper used in this book was obtained by unraveling the abaca from Ganpi Abaka Subaru knitting yarn by Noro. This requires a little patience as it can easily tear. Wind the abaca into a ball and retain the rest of the yarn for further use on a different project.

The hand-woven bag below was embroidered with this abaca paper. The tag depicting the robins was also embroidered in abaca paper on textured silk paper. The tag was backed onto brown leather.

The North Wind Doth Blow features a tag which, like the bag itself, is made from abaca paper on silk paper.

2 PAPER FROM FIBERS

Silk Papermaking

This method can be used with a selection of fibers to make a variety of papers. Try silk, linen, flax, merino tops, and rayon floss. Although the resulting fabric is referred to as paper, it really is a strong fabric that doesn't tear. Using different glues to bond the fibers produces different results. The papers in this book have been made using acrylic gloss medium, as the resulting papers are strong, durable, and waterproof. Try experimenting with the amount of glue you use as the results will vary dramatically.

Method

1. Spread plastic sheeting over the glue table to protect it.
2. Spread a sheet of netting on this.
3. Making sure that your hands are dry. Pull some fibers out of the silk hank.
4. Tease the fibers and pull them apart.
5. Lay them down on the netting, overlapping them in one direction and then another. (If you want the silk fabric to be lacy, just put one layer down.)
6. Place a second sheet of net over the fibers.
7. Mix up a solution of water and liquid dishwashing soap and paint this over the netting, letting it soak right through.
8. Pick the layers of net up and turn them over. Rub this side with the flat palms of your hand to make sure that the fibers inside are wet.
9. The sandwiched layers will be very soapy. Mix a solution of 8 teaspoons of water and 1 teaspoon of acrylic gloss medium for a soft and appealing fabric. (One part acrylic to four parts water for a stiffer fabric.)
10. Paint this on the soapy netting.
11. Use the flat palms of your hands to push and rub the solution into the fibers.
12. Turn the net over and repeat.
13. Hang the dripping net and fibers out to dry.
14. When it is dry, place it on a clean flat surface and carefully remove the netting. The netting can be retained and used each time you make paper.
15. Iron the silk.

TIPS
- To use this fabric for bag making, it should be covered with a silk sheer fabric to protect it (see bag, opposite).
- The bags in this book that require a firm fabric have been made from silk fibers bonded with a strong solution of at least one part acrylic to four parts water. These papers may not appear to be so attractive initially because they are firm, but this is a desirable quality for bag making.
- Many of the bags in this book that have been made from silk paper have a protective coating of acrylic wax, varnish, or beeswax polish.

YOU WILL NEED:
- silk fibers
- liquid dishwashing soap
- water
- a large brush
- acrylic gloss medium
- a teaspoon
- washing line and clothespins
- net
- plastic sheeting

Bag made with silk paper using degummed silk filament. Angelina fibers were used on top and a red silk sheer scarf placed over to prevent "bobbling" when in use.

Jester Bag

This bag, with its tiny decorative gold bells, is reminiscent of a medieval court jester's costume. It is made from degummed silk filament paper, which has been machine quilted.

YOU WILL NEED:

- 15½ x 16½ inch (40 x 42 cm) red silk paper
- 15½ x 16½ inch (40 x 42 cm) quilter's wadding with diagonal lines
- 15½ x 16½ inch (40 x 42 cm) yellow lining
- 15½ x 16½ inch (40 x 42 cm) red sheer fabric
- variegated machine embroidery thread, olive green
- 10 tiny bells
- tiny coordinating beads
- 40 inch (1 m) curly braid
- handles from a paper shopping bag
- olive green embroidery thread
- PVA glue
- 606 spray glue or fusible webbing
- 505 spray glue
- decorative bead or medallion
- 20 inches (50 cm) cord to crochet an edge (optional)
- baking parchment
- soldering iron

Method

1   To obtain the shape for the bag, draw a rectangle measuring 7½ x 7½ inches (19 x 19 cm) on scrap paper and round the bottom corners. Cut two.

2   Pin the patterns to the silk paper and cut out two pattern pieces. (Pin around the outside where the seam will go as all pin marks will show.)

3   Cut two batting pieces to size.

4   Use 505 Spray and Fix, repositionable spray glue to adhere the silk paper to the batting.

5   Turn the bag pieces over so that the red side is uppermost and spray 606 Spray and Fix glue over the red paper. You could use fusible webbing instead of 606, but 606 is preferable because it doesn't leave a shiny surface.

6   Place the sheer fabric over the glue side of the red paper, leaving a border of about ½ inch (1 cm) so that the sheer can be cut to size later. Place a sheet of baking parchment over the red paper and iron over the shapes. The sheer fabric will adhere to the fusible glue and this will be irreversible.

7   Use a soldering iron to cut the sheer fabric to the bag size and thus prevent it from fraying. (If you are not using a soldering iron, leave the sheer fabric border to prevent it from fraying.)

8   Use the variegated thread in the bobbin and on the top and set the machine to long stitch.

9   Place the fabric with the red side down and the batting facing you. Stitch in straight lines following the diagonals. Do this to both pieces.

10   Place the two right sides together and with a smaller stitch sew the sides, leaving the top open. Turn the bag the right side out.

11   Cut two pattern pieces of yellow lining to size.

12   Place the right sides together and sew round the sides, leaving the top open. Turn the top in ½ inch (1 cm). Iron it in place and set this aside until later.

13   If you wish, make a 20 inch (50 cm) chain of single crochet to go around the outside of the bag. With the flat side down, sew this crocheted braid to the outside seam of the bag.

14   Turn the top of the bag in about ½ inch (1 cm). Slip-stitch this in place.

Jester bag

The trimming

1 Cut a piece of batting as shown in the diagram. Bond the batting to red silk paper with 505 repositionable glue. Cover both sides of the batting and cut the red paper to size.

2 At this stage decide whether to cover the red paper trimming with the sheer fabric or whether to leave it as it is. Use buttonhole stitch to sew the edges together. (A smooth thread gives a neat formal appearance. A viscose loopy thread gives it a bit more life.) Embroider around the outside edge using an olive green decorative thread and add beads.

3 Sew the bells to the tip of each point.

4 Sew the zigzag trimming to the top of the bag.

5 Stitch the curly braid to the top of the bag. Use two rows of braid to give it extra body. Stitch one row to the inside and one row to the outside of the bag.

6 Sew the decorative bead or medallion in place in the center of the bag.

7 If you wish, sew crocheted trimming to the top of the bag.

The handles

1 Take the brown paper shopping bag and carefully remove the handles by tearing out the card encasing the handles. By retaining the card you are adding strength to the bag handles.

2 Trim the card to fit the bag. Wrap the olive green thread round the handles.

TIP: A thin embroidery thread looks good but is more time consuming. The thickness of the thread determines the ultimate appearance and character of the bag. It is easier to wrap the handles if you anchor one end down with masking tape. If it becomes necessary to join the thread, use double-sided tape.

3 Now take the handles and fit them in the bag. Measure the distance from the sides and mark the inside of the bag on the batting as a guide for sticking. Cover one side of the card encasing the handles with PVA glue and carefully insert it into the bag. Check the position to be certain that it is correct before it is too late to rectify it. Before gluing the next handle, insert that into the bag and check which way around looks best. Take this handle out and cover the card surrounding it with PVA glue. Carefully insert this handle into the bag, lining it up with the first handle. Leave these to dry.

4 Finally, insert the yellow lining into the bag and slip-stitch it in place.

Cocoon stripping tub bag with a Softsculpt impressed badge.

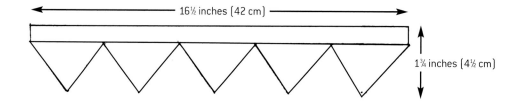

PROJECT

Glitterati Fusible Film and Peeled Paint Distress Embossing Powders

This bag causes a stir wherever it goes because no one can work out what it is made from. The base fabric for this bag is silk paper made with one part acrylic gloss medium to four parts water. One advantage is that this fabric remains easy to stitch into.

Method

1   Cut the silk paper to size.
2   Use heat-fixable paint in blue and green to paint the paper. While it is still wet, sprinkle blue embossing powder and green peeled paint distress embossing powder over it. (You will need to use quite a large amount of peeled paint distress powder to cover the whole bag.)
3   Heat using a heat tool.
4   Place Stewart Gill iridescent Glitterati fusible film over the embossed silk and place a sheet of baking parchment over it to protect your iron.
5   Iron to bond the film until it distresses and shrinks back to reveal the embossing underneath. (Watch carefully to ensure you do not burn too much back.)
6   The handles for this bag were enameled. Cover each handle with heat-fixable paint, sprinkle Opalette embossing enamels on and heat with a heat tool.

Further examples of combining heat-fixable paint with distress powders can be seen on page 125.

YOU WILL NEED:
- silk paper
- blue and green heat-fixable paint
- embossing powder
- heat tool
- Stewart Gill iridescent Glitterati fusible film
- baking parchment
- ready-made handles
- Opalette enamel powder

Glitterati and peeled paint on silk paper. This is a detail of the Glitterati bag shown on page 6.

Leather-effect Silk Paper

Dyeing with ferrous sulphate is an exciting experience. To obtain a rich rust color, follow the method below but take note of the safety precautions as the solution does stain! Make sure you use an old saucepan, wear a respirator and mask because of the fumes and open all windows. Protect your hands with rubber gloves. Protect the drying area.

The method may seem rather drastic but the end results make it worthwhile. The resulting fabric remains easy to stitch into and so either sparse or intensive embroidery can be worked on it.

The silk paper for the bag opposite was first stamped into and embossed with powder prior to dyeing. The dyeing process "knocked back" the embossing. When it was dry, it was ironed, and this began to improve the appearance. A coat of acrylic wax was then painted on and allowed to dry. A liberal coat of beeswax polish ensured that the paper was sealed. The paper does not resemble leather until all the steps described below have been followed.

This project shows just how robust silk paper made with one part acrylic gloss medium to four parts water can be.

Method
1   Place 9 ounces (250 g) ferrous sulphate in a pan, kept exclusively for dyeing.
2   Add 2 quarts (2 liters) of water and heat gently to dissolve the crystals.
3   Add the fabric and bring to the boil. Boil for 10 minutes.
4   Remove the fabric and spread it out to dry outside.
5   Dissolve ¼ ounce (5 g) bicarbonate of soda in warm water.
6   Place the fabric in this solution for 10 minutes, rinse thoroughly in cold water, then dry.
7   Iron the fabric.
8   Wax it with acrylic wax and when this is dry, polish it with beeswax polish.

Opposite: Ca d'Oro Palace leather effect silk paper bag with an appliqued cocoon stripping panel.

Right: Detail from the front panel of the bag.

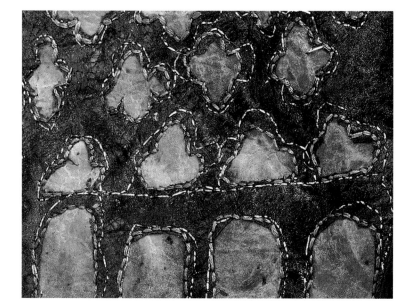

Leather-effect Bag made from Silk Paper Scraps

Keep all of the silk paper scraps you will have left when you cut out patterns. They can be reconstituted by sandwiching them between two large pieces of net and, by using the same glue from which the scraps were first made, another sheet of paper can be formed. This second sheet will be more like card stock as it will have had two doses of glue added to it. It will, however, be very strong and can be used to make bags or tags.

Reconstituted silk paper bonded to Softsculpt. The bag features a shrink-plastic tag and glue-gun brooch.

Reconstituted Silk Papers

The silk paper used to make the bag opposite had blue and green Stewart Gill Byzantia heat-fixable paint applied in some areas. When the reconstituted silk paper was dyed using ferrous sulphate, this "knocked back" the strong color and made it more muted. The paper looked most unappealing until it was ironed. After this it was possible to see that parts of it were lacy and open. This was great for a distressed appearance.

It was bonded to a sheet of Softsculpt with 505 repositionable glue, and the exposed areas were heated. A rubber stamp with a vermicelli design was then pressed into the warm Softsculpt (sometimes sold as Formafoam).

The fabric was given a coat of acrylic wax. When this was dry, beeswax clear polish was gently rubbed in. (This smells at first but wears off.)

The fabric was embroidered using a meandering vermicelli pattern on the sewing machine. Stitch-and-Tear on the back of the Softsculpt made the machining easier.

In this *Bubble and Squeak* bag (below), the fish motifs were cut from Translucent Liquid Sculpey (TLS) paper, which was made with two layers of liquid (see page 107). It was colored with alcohol inks and embroidered on the matt side. The pattern was drawn on with a gold gel pen.

I call this bag *Bubble and Squeak* because it is made from leftover silk paper. My husband says it could equally be called "Fish and Sticks".

Pre-dyed Silk Paper

To obtain the desired effect the silk paper was dyed by boiling it in ferrous sulphate. It is not the same color as the bag on page 37 because the silk paper had already been painted before it went into the dyepot. (If you want pure rust color, then put white silk paper that has not been colored into the dyepot.) When the fabric comes out of the dye pot it will look very crumpled but ironing the dry fabric transforms it. It will not resemble leather until it has been waxed.

A store-bought stamp was used to apply the pattern on this fabric. It was embossed with embossing powder and then painted with Stewart Gill heat-fixable paint. When this was dry, it was given a coat of acrylic wax. The fabric was embroidered and beaded.

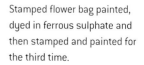

Stamped flower bag painted, dyed in ferrous sulphate and then stamped and painted for the third time.

Two sticks were sanded and colored with Procion dye. See safety instructions that come with dyes and seal dyed sticks with varnish or polyurethane. Silk carrier rods were used to support the stick handles. These silk strips are quite robust. They make good supports for stick handles as they are easy to stitch into. They have a wonderful gnarled texture resembling the bark from trees. In use they have a tendency to get pills. In order to overcome this, it is necessary to strengthen them. There are three ways in which to do this:

1 Paint them with a solution of PVA mixed with water.
2 Paint them with Ormoline (available from online sources outside the United States).
3 Paint them with acrylic wax.

Red Leather-effect Silk Paper

Making the fabric resemble leather using this method relies heavily on the application of acrylic wax, encaustic wax, and beeswax polish (or clear furniture polish).

Method
1 Begin by making the silk paper.
2 Mix red acrylic paint with Ormoline and paint it on the silk paper.
3 When this is dry, iron red encaustic wax onto the paper.
4 Paint a layer of acrylic wax over the paper.
5 When this is dry, rub beeswax furniture polish into the paper and buff it until the paper shines.

Red leather-effect bag
decorated with style stones.

Animal-stamped, leather-effect silk bag.

Blue Leather-effect Silk Paper

Method

1 Make some silk paper, ensuring you have enough for the size required.
2 The animal stamp was made by drawing the image onto Funky Foam and cutting it out using a soldering iron. Some pattern was etched onto the body. (Remember to take safety precautions when using the soldering iron.)
3 Use your stamp with Stazon ink and emboss with green distressing peeled paint embossing powder.
4 Outline the images in backstitch, using blue variegated cotton.
5 Now paint the background with blue acrylic paint. Apply interference oxide green in some areas.
6 The stamp-embossed shapes can be painted with Byzantia Excelsius paint and then parts rubbed off right away to reveal the layers underneath.
7 Iron blue encaustic wax on to the blue areas.
8 Paint acrylic wax over the whole fabric.
9 Apply a final layer of wax polish liberally and buff to a sheen.

Cocoon Strippings

Method

1   Place a sheet of baking parchment on the ironing board.
2   Pull a small amount of cocoon fibers out and tease them to pull them apart.
3   Repeat and lay them side by side until you have enough to make the size of paper you require. Do not make thick layers at this stage. If you do, you may find that the fibers will not bond successfully.
4   Pour some water into a plastic travel spray bottle. Spray the water onto the gummed cocoon strippings.
5   Cover the strippings with another sheet of baking parchment.
6   Iron the strippings until they are dry. You will end up with a thin lacy sheet of paper.
7   If you want the paper to be robust, place another layer of teased strippings on top, spray with water, and iron over the baking parchment again.
8   When you have the required thickness of paper, mix a solution of 1 teaspoon of Ormoline with 4 teaspoons of water and paint this on the paper.
9   If you require a firm paper, a coat of acrylic wax could be used or PVA could be diluted with water.
10 A coat of furniture polish gives extra protection if required. You might also consider using a coat of varnish or even nail polish. Silk sheers on top of the paper sometimes can be very effective.

Cocoon stripping paper with burned back sheers. A glue-gun motif decorates the center.

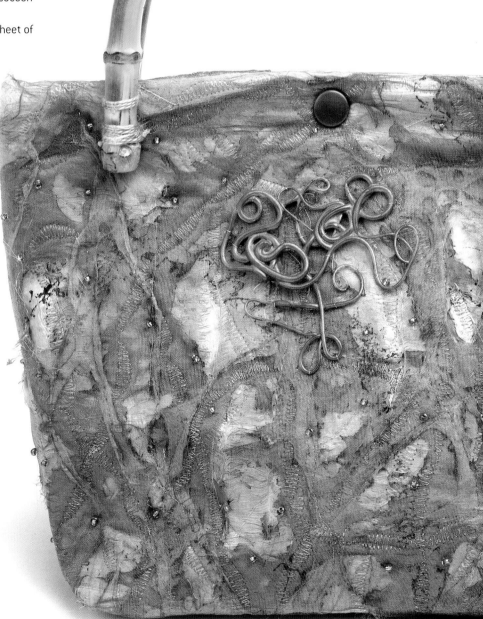

Fabrics with Distressed Embossing Enamels

The style and inspiration for the fabric on the opposite page came from a painting by John Waterhouse called *Miranda, The Tempest*. The fabric for the bag was intended to look old and worn like an old saddle bag.

Method

1   Make silk paper from cocoon strippings.
2   Color with a solution of coffee and water and leave it to dry.
3   Paint acrylic wax over the coffee solution to seal it.
4   When this was dry, gently rub in lots of beeswax polish.
5   Bond the paper to wadding (I used 505, repositional glue). The best batting to use is for quilters and has diagonal lines on the back. This made it easy to embroider the lines in Sorbello stitch.
6   Heat-fixable paint by Stewart Gill can be applied in some areas and triple embossing enamels sprinkled on and heated. The layers can be deliberately made thick and, when it is cool, pieces can be cracked and chipped off to expose the paint underneath.

TIP: Keep the pieces to use on another project, as the enamel can be reheated and reused.

The fabric fro this bag has been distressed to give a saddle-bag effect.

3 TEXTURED PAPERS

YOU WILL NEED:

- onion skins
- tissue paper, brown paper, white paper
- cotton linters
- water
- jug
- blender
- large deep tray
- deckle (or wire mesh)
- newspapers
- two large wooden boards
- kitchen cloths

The exciting thing about working with pulp papers is that you never really know how each batch will work out. The overriding rule is that you only get out what you put in! If you only put tissue paper in the vat, this is what you will get out. If you only put card in, then, again, this is what you will get out. The secret, therefore, is to put a good mixture of textures in so that something unique comes out. Pulp paper that is suitable for embroidery really needs to have cotton linters added to make the paper feel more like felt. Brown paper is often a good source of pulp paper. If it is going to be painted it won't matter if the resulting pulp is unappealing in color. Avoid using any glossy magazines or newspapers as these really do not make good pulp. Also, if you add anything with a hint of color, the whole batch of pulp papers will be discolored, although of course sometimes this doesn't matter, depending on your project.

Because each paper is unique it's a good idea to keep a record of what you have done in case you want to repeat it. Generally speaking, the longer you press your paper the stronger it becomes. It does however become flatter and smoother if you press it and dry it for a long period. You need to bear this in mind if you want to add texture and character. You could try drying it over bubble wrap, net, plant material, and any raised surfaces, or try trapping materials in it.

For bag making, pulp paper needs to be thought of as a panel since it is not pliable enough to use any other way. For example, the bag on page 47 uses two panels of pulp paper with onion skins added to provide the texture. The knobbly texture is further enhanced by stitching and beading. You need to make two sheets of onion paper 8 x 10 inches (20 x 25 cm).

Onion Skin Paper

1   Collect onion skins until a lightweight plastic food bag is three-quarters full.
2   Tear brown paper, tissue paper, and white paper (not newspapers or glossy magazines) into pieces about the size of stamps. Tear up a quarter of a page of cotton linters.
3   Soak all the paper and the onion skins in boiling water and leave to soak for a few hours.

A

B

C

4   Prepare the equipment for the next stage so that everything is on hand: a jug of warm water, a blender, a deckle, and a tray large enough the take the deckle. (If you do not have a deckle, a sheet of wire mesh will do. Make sure the edges are not sharp and cover them with masking tape.)

5   Spoon the paper and water mixture into the blender a little at a time. Pour warm water into the blender and replace the lid. Blend this mixture, making sure it doesn't stick to the blades. If it sticks or makes a straining noise, turn it off and add more water (A).

6   Pour the pulp paper mixture into the tray and repeat until you have blended all of the pulp paper (B).

7   You will now have a tray with very thick pulp and water. The onion skins will have broken up but will still retain some texture and character.

8   Carefully slide the deckle into the tray and wiggle it about to let the pulp paper settle on the mesh (C).

9   Spread the newspaper on a wooden board outside.

10 Place a kitchen cloth on the newspapers.

11 Invert the pulp onto the kitchen cloth. It is best to tip it out in one quick, smooth action. If it breaks up or folds in on itself, tip it back into the pulp vat and start again. (d)

12 Place another kitchen cloth on top of the pulp and repeat until all the pulp is used up. When you reach your final layer, place another kitchen cloth on it. (Each sheet of paper should have a kitchen cloth on either side to prevent the sheets from sticking.)

13 To speed up the drying process you need to squeeze out as much water as you can. Place another board on top and a heavy weight if you have one (E). A lot of water will come out. Standing on the board squeezes water out, but it is best to have someone holding on to you as the pile of paper is very slippery.

14 Leave the papers to dry. When the water has stopped running, place the papers somewhere warm to dry completely.

D   E

Coloring the paper

Pulp paper is very porous and any paint applied tends to have a flat, dull appearance that is not attractive. There are two ways in which to overcome this.

1   Mix PVA glue with water and apply a coat of this solution to the untreated paper. Wait until it is dry before coloring it. This method will obtain a varnished appearance.
2   Alternatively, color the paper with paint. When it is dry, give it a coat of acrylic wax.

The paper for the onion skin bag (opposite) was colored with crimson copper bronzing powder mixed with acrylic wax. Remember to wear a respirator and mask and work in a well-ventilated area for this stage. When the bronzing powder and wax were dry, black webbing spray was used. It is a good idea to work outside so that you do not breathe in the fumes. Antique copper bronzing powder was then mixed with acrylic sand texture gel and acrylic wax. A roller was used to lightly cover the raised areas on the paper. A little patination fluid was then dabbed on with a paintbrush. Pearl-Ex paint was applied sparingly to one or two areas.

Embroidering the paper

For the bag, cut a rectangle measuring 8 x 5½ inches (20 x 14 cm) out of the colored onion skin pulp paper. This will be on the bag front. Then cut out a square measuring 5½ x 5½ inches (14 x 14 cm). This will be on the front flap. Use 505 spray glue to attach panels of thin fabric to the back of the pulp papers. This will give extra stability to the stitches.

Use threads of varying thickness to stitch into the peaks and troughs in the paper. Masking tape can be used to anchor the end of the thread down on the back as it will not be seen afterwards. French knots and Sorbello stitch work well if used in varying sizes.

Onion Skin Paper Bag

Method

1 If your fabric frays, serge the edges on the sewing machine.
2 Take the front pattern piece and the 8½ x 5½ inches (20 x 14 cm) pulp paper and use 505 spray glue to position the pulp paper on the fabric. You need to leave a border of ⅜ inch (1 cm) for the seam allowance and ⅜ inch (1 cm) for framing. The top will have a larger border at this stage so that you have plenty of room to maneuver when it is turned in.
3 Use the thick thread or chenille wool to embroider around the edge of the panel in Sorbello stitch. The embroidery often looks more appealing if it begins on the paper and encroaches onto the fabric.
4 Take the front flap pattern piece and the remaining pulp paper pattern piece that has been embroidered. Repeat the process above and appliqué the paper to the fabric.
5 Next take the front and back patterns and place the right sides together. Sew around the sides and base leaving the top open.
6 Carefully turn the bag inside out.
7 Press with an iron without going over the pulp paper.
8 Turn the top in.
9 Take the front and back flap and put the right sides together. Sew round the three sides, leaving the top open. Taper the two sides at the top slightly so that when you fit it into the bag it isn't too bulky.
10 Pin and tack the flap to the back of the bag and then sew it in place.
11 Turn the edges of the strap in ⅜ inch (1 cm) at both sides. Iron this in place. Put the two sides together and with a matching thread sew down the side so that the strap measures ¾ inch (2 cm) wide.
12 Position the strap to the inside of the bag and sew both sides in place.
13 Cut out two pattern pieces in lining material, 9½ x 7 inches (24 x 18 cm).
14 Sew the lining together leaving the top open.
15 Insert the lining into the bag and slip-stitch it into place.

YOU WILL NEED:

- embroidered onion skin paper panels (see opposite)
- 2 rectangles 9½ x 7 inches (24 x18 cm) matching fabric for the back and front
- 2 rectangles 8 x 7 inches (20 x 18 cm) matching fabric for the flap
- a strip 39½ x 2¾ inches (1 m x 6 cm) matching fabric for the strap
- 505 spray glue
- chenille wool or a thick thread for the border
- 2 rectangles 24 x 8cm (9½ x 7 inches) lining material
- matching machine sewing thread
- pins

Onion skin bag.

Silk Paper, Paper Perfect, and TLS Tiles

This bag is called *Oh, I Do Like to be Beside the Seaside* because of the images used to decorate the sides. The shower-curtain handle completes the nautical theme.

To make the paper for this bag a sheet of silk paper was made with acrylic gloss medium (one part acrylic medium and four parts water). The silk paper was cut to size and then covered with Paper Perfect, a ready-made pulp mixture that is sold for stampers and scrapbook makers. It comes in a jar in a range of colors, but the color is not important as it will be covered with paint for this project. Simply open the jar and spread the thick mixture on the silk paper using a spatula and then it is ready to dry. Drying can take one to two days. The silk paper for the seaside bag was then colored with Stewart Gill Byzantia Fra Angelico heat-fixable paint. When this was dry it was painted with acrylic wax. The tiles and tag were made from Translucent Liquid Sculpey (TLS). The images were stamped on the sheet of TLS and a second layer of TLS was applied and baked. (See page 107 for more on working with TLS.) The handle for the bag is made from the links sold for use with a shower curtain.

Paper Perfect over Embossed Copper Shim

Images can be transferred to pulp paper by drying it over embossed copper and the resulting paper can be made into a bag. Paper Perfect is very simple to use for this technique. Sew the seams with the insides together as it will not be robust enough to turn the bag inside out.

Method

1   Draw your design on tracing paper.
2   Attach the tracing to a sheet of copper shim with masking tape.
3   Transfer the design to the copper using an embossing tool.
4   Remove the tracing and continue to add depth to the piece by using different-sized embossing tools.
5   Cover the back of the copper with a thin layer of Vaseline.
6   Use a spatula to spread the Paper Perfect over the Vaseline. (Any color will do as you will be coloring the finished pulp paper when it is dry.)
7   Leave it to dry.
8   When it is dry, remove it from the copper shim.
9   The paper can now be painted and the embossed shim can be washed to remove the Vaseline. (The copper can be reused for other projects.)
10 Bond the colored paper to batting with repositionable glue before you stitch into it.

The same design was drawn onto soluble fabric to make the free-machine lace for this bag.

Bag made with Paper Perfect and machine lace.

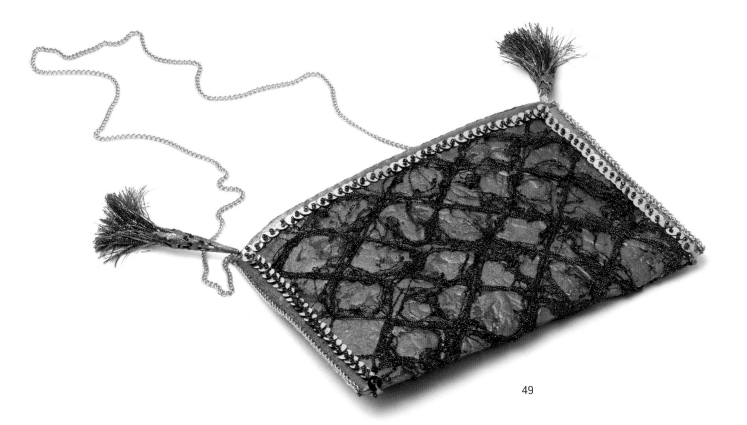

Sinamay and Paper Perfect

Sinamay is a mesh of woven plant fiber often used in millinery.

1   Place the sinamay over silk paper. (I used de-gummed silk filament paper, which I had colored in red and brown.)
2   Use a palette knife to spread Paper Perfect over the sinamay.
3   Allow this to dry.
4   Color the paper. (I used Stewart Gill Byzantia Excelsius.)
5   When it is dry, apply a coat of acrylic wax.
6   When the wax is dry, rub beeswax polish into the paper.
7   Add color by applying alcohol inks with a cosmetic sponge. (Blending fluid may be helpful if you use more than one color.)

Tip: If you do not like the effect it can be "knocked back" with blending fluid.

8   Finally, varnish the paper with clear nail varnish or a varnish glaze.

The texture of the fabric was effective. As it is very rigid, the bag was made up with the insides together so that it did not need to be turned inside out. The fabric makes a really sturdy, robust bag, which can be stitched into. A paper clay motif was made to go in the center. The paper clay was colored with the same alcohol inks and sewn in position.

Lascaux Sinamay bag.

Tangle Tuff and Paper Perfect

Tangle Tuff is similar to sinamay, in that it is an open-weave mesh, but it has swirling patterns. Paper Perfect applied to any textured paper surface works well and—when applied to Tangle Tuff fibers—it reminded me of tangled undergrowth, so that became the theme for this bag.

1   Place the sheet of Tangle Tuff over a sheet of silk paper.
2   Use a palette knife to apply the Paper Perfect to the fibers.
3   Leave it to dry.
4   Color the dried paper with Stewart Gill Byzantia Excelsius paint.
5   When this is dry, apply interference oxide green in certain areas.
6   Spray with black webbing spray. (Do this outside with the ground protected.)
7   Paint acrylic wax over the paper.
8   Use a cosmetic sponge to apply alcohol inks.
9   Bead and stitch the fabric.
10 Cut the fabric to size and make up into a bag.

Do not put the right sides together as it is too brittle to be turned inside out. The flower is made out of paper clay and is colored with Stewart Gill Byzantia Excelsius.

This bag is called *Tangled Undergrowth*.

Rustic newspaper bag.

Rustic Newspaper Bag

This bag has been created from layers of newspaper and furnishing fabric, aged and distressed to give an organic effect. Handles made from sticks complete the natural look. Finding the right furnishing fabric is the key to this project; you need a design that is loosely woven or has long threads on the back that can be cut and distressed. The antique-looking seal, made from glue and a rubber stamp, adds a finishing touch.

Making the fabric

1   Color the sheet of newspaper using a sponge soaked in cold coffee. Leave to dry.
2   Place the sheet of newspaper onto the back of the furnishing fabric and cut away any excess fabric.
3   Drop the feed dog on the sewing machine, and sew the newspaper to the back of the furnishing fabric using straight stitch in meandering vertical lines. Make the lines fairly close together and overlap them (A).
4   Using a metal brush or teasel, pull or tear pieces of paper away (B and C). You may need to tear the paper by hand but don't be tempted to use scissors as they will make the edges look too neat. Draw through some of the threads from the fabric underneath and distress the whole surface, using scissors to cut any long threads on the fabric (D, overleaf).
5   Place protective newspaper on a flat surface in a well-ventilated area. Place the fabric onto the newspaper, turn newspaper side up and lightly cover with black webbing spray.
6   If the fabric looks appealing at this stage, then proceed with making the bag. If it lacks character, then you need to work into it some more. Try handsewing in running stitch or backstitch, or place a dyed diaper liner over the fabric, stitch into it, and blast it with a heat tool. A potential problem with this method is that it can feel hard to the touch so try it out on a scrap piece first.

MATERIALS
- 11 x 17¼ inches (28 x 44 cm) sheet of newspaper
- sponge
- coffee granules
- 1 piece furnishing fabric, 12 x 20 inches (30 x 50 cm)
- scissors
- sewing machine
- metal brush or teasel
- extra newspaper for protection
- black webbing spray
- felt lining fabric, 12 x 20 inches (30 x 50 cm)
- craft knife
- 2 interesting sticks, about 8¾ inches (22 cm) for the handles
- sandpaper
- baking parchment or Teflon baking tray
- talcum powder
- hot-glue gun
- rubber stamp
- bronzing powder
- Ormoline fabric medium
- patination fluid
- metallic cotton thread

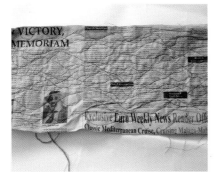

A

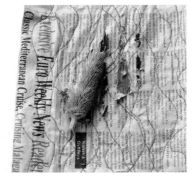

B

C

53

Making the bag

1   Cut four strips out of the resulting fabric, 1¼ x 7 inches (3 x 18 cm) each. Then cut out a piece of fabric for the main bag, 8¼ x 12½ inches (21 x 32 cm).
2   Fold the main piece in half, newspaper sides together, and then sew up the two sides with a ⅜ inch (1 cm) seam allowance. Turn the bag inside out and fray the top edge by picking at it with a pair of embroidery scissors.
3   Cut out the felt lining material and fold it into the shape of the bag. Sew the two sides together. Do not insert it yet.

Making the handles

1   Use a craft knife to strip the bark off the sticks and then sandpaper them until smooth.
2   Insert the two strips of the fabric into the bag, about 1¼ inch (3 cm) in at each end of the top opening. Sew them in place using the sewing machine.

Making the seal

1   Spread out a sheet of baking parchment or use a Teflon baking tray and dust the rubber stamp with talcum powder (F).
2   Insert a glue stick into the glue gun and when it has heated up squeeze the trigger to make a patch of glue. Be careful not to touch the glue with your fingers as it will be very hot. After five seconds, push the rubber stamp into the glue and leave it there until the glue is cold. Remove the stamp from the glue—you will be left with an uneven, irregular impression that helps give the illusion of age (G).
3   Working in a well-ventilated area, wearing a respirator and mask, mix ¼ teaspoon bronzing powder with ½ teaspoon Ormoline fabric medium. Paint the resulting mixture onto the glue patch. To give an aged appearance, paint little touches of patination fluid onto the patch while the bronzing powder paint is still wet.

TIP: Be sparing with patination fluid—it only shows up when it is dry.

4   When the patch is dry, you can stitch into it with metallic thread but be careful not to tear the glue. Running stitch and backstitch are suitable stitches for this. Once you have decorated it to your satisfaction, stitch it carefully to the center front of the bag (H).

D

E

Finishing the bag

1 Insert the lining into the bag, and sew it in.
2 Finally, slide the two sticks through the tabs and stitch them in position so that they do not move about.

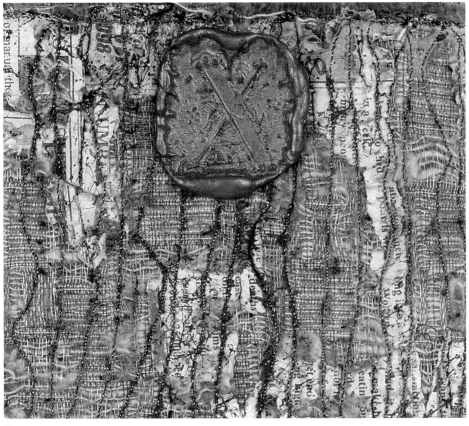

H

F   G

Malachite and Azurite Shoulder Bag

This bag was inspired by rocks I found in Spain. It is made out of brown paper and can be adapted to fit any size.

YOU WILL NEED:

- brown paper shopping bag
- blue webbing spray
- black sheer, 18 x 9 inches (46 x 23 cm)
- blue lining, 18 x 9 inches (46 x 23 cm)
- curtain interlining or wadding of your choice, 18 x 9 inches (46 x 23 cm)
- 505 repositionable spray glue
- 51 inches (130 cm) compressed paper cord
- beads, wool, ribbons, and embroidery threads
- yarn to wrap the handle
- metallic machine embroidery thread
- gold bronzing powder
- Ormoline or acrylic wax
- blue and brown Brusho (U.K. watercolor pigment available from online sources) or other water-based pigment powders
- double-sided sticky tape
- masking tape
- heat gun
- brooch (optional)

Method

1. Open out a shopping bag and dab small patches of azure blue Brusho paint on the brown paper. Paint brown Brusho paint in some areas.
2. Mix gold bronzing powder with either Ormoline or acrylic wax and paint this in large areas. Wear a respirator and mask and work in a well-ventilated area. Wipe up any spillage of powder with a wet tissue.
3. Check that all the paper is covered with the three colors and wait until it is dry.
4. Take the colored paper outside and spread newspapers to protect the ground. Use blue webbing spray sparingly (see A, below) and when it is dry, crumple the paper up as hard as you can (see B, below).
5. Open the paper and without smoothing it out too much, cover it with the black sheer fabric.
6. Tack around the edges of the paper.
7. Use a metallic thread to stitch randomly into these layers. Stitch with the feed dog down.
8. Wearing a respirator and mask, burn back the sheer fabric.
9. Use 505 spray glue to attach the paper to the interlining.
10. Use beads, wool, threads, and ribbons to embroider the bag. Knobbly stitches like French knots and Sorbello work well.
11. Fold the bag in half and sew around the two sides with the right sides together and leaving the top open.
12. Turn the bag the other way out so that the embroidery is showing.
13. Fold the lining in half and sew around the two sides.
14. Turn the top of the bag in ⅜ inch (1 cm), and slip-stitch it in place.

A

B

15 Turn the top of the lining in, and iron it in place.
16 Use masking tape to anchor the ends of the yarn to the compressed paper cord and wrap the paper cord. Use double-sided tape if joins are needed.
17 Insert the ends in the corners of the bag and sew them in place.
18 Attach a brooch now if you are using one.
19 Insert the lining and slip-stitch it in place.

Copper and Black
Machine-embroidered Bag

To make the fabric

1 Take a sheet of brown paper and paint the whole sheet with black fabric paint.
2 Allow the paint to dry and then paint large semicircular shapes on the paper using black acrylic paint.
3 When this is dry, highlight the acrylic paint with the acrylic wax.
4 When the paper is completely dry, take it in your hands and crumple it up as hard as you can.

TIP: The aim of the next stage is to strengthen the paper and to obtain an appropriate weight for the bag.

5 Draw the basic pattern for the bag on scrap paper (see diagram, below).
6 Cut this paper pattern out and pin it to the batting.
7 Cut the batting to fit the pattern.
8 Use 505 spray glue to bond the batting to the Stitch and Tear.
9 Cut out the Stitch and Tear to fit the pattern shape.
10 Use 505 spray glue to bond the painted, crumpled paper to the batting.
11 Cut out the crumpled paper leaving a border of about 1⅛ inch (3 cm) (see A, below).
12 Place the black sheer fabric over the crumpled paper.
13 Attach the sheer by stitching along the outside edges using long machine stitch.
14 Add character to the piece by dropping the feed dog and using free-machine embroidery to lightly cover the surface. Use a metallic heat-resistant thread on the top and in the bobbin. Meander in a loose way and do not densely cover the fabric. Leave the Stitch and Tear in place.
15 Work in a well-ventilated area and wear a respirator and mask. Use a heat tool to burn back the sheer. Watch carefully so that you are in control of the amount to be burned back.
16 Still wearing the mask, mix a heaped teaspoon of the sand texture gel, the heavy gloss medium and ½ teaspoon of copper bronzing powder.
17 Tear the masking tape into irregular shaped strips and stick them onto the painted fabric in roughly shaped diagonal lines.
18 Lightly use a roller (brayer) to apply the bronze paint to the fabric (see B, below). Start with the center stripe and leave a slight gap between each line of rolling.
19 When the paint is dry, peel off the masking tape.
20 Trim the crumpled paper and sheer fabric to fit the bag pattern (see C, overleaf).

YOU WILL NEED:

- brown paper, 16 x 13 inches (40 x 33 cm)
- wadding, 16 x 13 inches (40 x 33 cm)
- Stitch and Tear fabric stabilizer, 16 x 13 inches (40 x 33 cm)
- black lining, 16 x 13 inches (40 x 33 cm)
- 25½ inches (65 cm) black velvet ribbon ⅜ inch (1 cm) wide
- 31½ inches (80 cm) black tubing
- 4 silk cocoons
- black sewing cotton
- 1½ inch (4 cm) masking tape
- black Velcro, or a magnetic fastener
- black acrylic paint
- black fabric paint
- acrylic wax
- natural sand texture gel
- gloss heavy medium gel
- copper bronzing powder
- sheer black fabric
- heat-resistant machine embroidery thread, black/silver
- 505 spray glue
- roller
- small beads

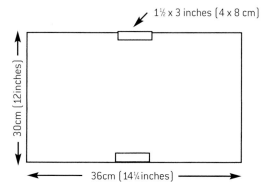

1½ x 3 inches (4 x 8 cm)

30cm (12inches)

36cm (14¼inches)

A

21 With the right sides together, sew up the two sides of the bag.
22 Go to the base of the bag and push the side seam in to meet the center of the cut-out rectangle. Stitch across this line. Do this to both sides.
23 Turn the bag inside out.

The handles

1 Check that the silk cocoons fit on the end of the tubing. Paint them with acrylic black paint and leave them to dry.
2 When the cocoons are dry, you can leave them as they are or embroider into them. To embroider into them use buttonhole stitch. Start at the open base and remember not to crisscross the thread inside the cocoon as this would prevent the tube from fitting in the cocoon.
3 Sew beads on.
4 Take the black tubing and cut it in two. Check that the length is suitable. The tubing needs to be pliable and easy to stitch into. (Black plastic tubing used to cover outside wires is suitable. The tubing used on some foot pumps can also be used.)
5 Take the silk cocoons and fit them onto the ends of the tubing. You may not need glue but if you do a little PVA will suffice.
6 Attach the cocoon and tube together by sewing and winding the embroidery thread around the first ring.
7 Mark the sewing position on the inside of the bag on each side.
8 Using strong sewing cotton, sew the handles on, wrapping the cotton around the first ring only so that it looks neat.

The lining

1 Cut the same rectangular pattern out in lining material.
2 Put the right sides together and sew it up in the same way as the bag.
3 Cut a 1⅛-inch (3-cm) strip of black Velcro and sew it to the center of the lining on each side. Alternatively attach magnetic fasteners.
4 Sew a button or decorative piece on the front of the bag.
5 Insert the lining into the bag and pull the top of it over the bag so that it wraps over the front.
6 Handstitch the lining to the bag front so that no stitches can be seen inside.
7 Sew the velvet ribbon onto the front of the bag so that it looks decorative and it covers the lining on the bag front. It should be easy to sew on the sewing machine as the tubing handles are very flexible.

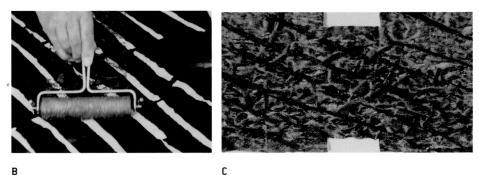

B   C

Liquid Appliqué

This multilayered fabric was inspired by an original design by Xantha Rottner.
The fabric for this bag came about after considerable experimentation. Playing around with simple shapes, different papers, and paint finishes can produce pleasing results. The fabric for this bag only came to life when the liquid appliqué was applied and this prompted the wheat sheaf theme. It then became easy to see which thread and stitch to use to decorate it.

Try

1   Tearing and cutting simple shapes out of different types of paper. You could use cartridge paper (heavy drawing paper), tissue paper, silk paper, newspaper, or textured papers.

2   Play around with the shapes on your chosen background paper.

3   When you are satisfied with the basic design, bond the shapes to the paper. You could use any glue at this experimental stage.

4   Stitch into the shapes either by hand or by machine.

5   Experiment with different paints to see which finish you prefer. Paint over the stitches.

6   Cover the paper with patterned or plain colored sheer fabric. This bag (right) was covered with white silk so that the papers and stitching underneath became shadowy.

7   Consider painting the sheer fabric.

8   Apply puff paint like Xpandaprint, Filigree Fluid or Liquid Appliqué. Use a heat tool to puff up the paint. Try coloring the puff paint, or you could buy it ready colored as shown in this bag.

9   Experiment with threads and stitching prior to embarking on your project.

10 Bond the paper to batting or felt and then stitch into it.

Wheat Sheaf bag.

4 COLOR AND PATTERN

Color and Pattern with Bonded Patches

The fabric for this bag is quite complex as multiple layers of fabrics are sandwiched together to achieve the desired effect.

Method

1   Layer five fabrics; curtain interlining for the base, painted bookbinder's tissue, Angelina fibers, blue metallic mesh, gold sheer fabric.
2   Add tramlines to the fabric by sewing two parallel lines in a grid formation.
3   Use a soldering iron to remove the resulting squares of gold sheer fabric (you can keep the squares to use on another project).
4   Paint selected squares with acrylic paint, then crackle glaze, and gold interference paint. Add a final layer of color was added with alcohol inks.
5   Mylar Shimmer Sheetz beads can be colored in the same way (A).
6   Place colored sheers on top of Kunin felt and use a soldering iron to burn into them and bond them together. These squares can be appliquéd to the alternate unpainted areas (B).
7   The store-bought handles were wrapped with yarn and tassels were made to act as a focal point for the center of the bag.
8   Add handles. The trimming around the top of the bag and the seams is made from knitted ribbon. Rug wool was threaded through the turbular ribbon and the ribbon was pulled up so it became ruffled.

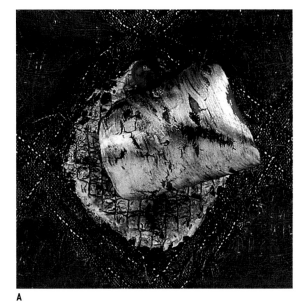

A

B

Trapping Leaves and Petals with Fusible Webbing

This method is often unpredictable—however carefully you position the petals they always move a little, giving the piece a charming spontaneity.

Method

1   Color the paper.
2   Place the dry colored paper between sheets of baking parchment to protect the ironing board and iron from the glue.
3   Cut a piece of fusible webbing to size. Peel the gauze off the backing paper and place it on the colored paper. Position the items that are to be trapped, such as flowers, petals, or other items, onto this layer.
4   Cut another layer of fusible webbing to size and peel this layer of gauze off.
5   Place this over the layers on the ironing board.
6   Cut sheer fabric to size and place this on top.
7   Protect this multilayered pile with another sheet of baking parchment.
8   Iron the whole piece with the iron set on a low heat.

Rose petal bridesmaid's bag.

The temperature of the iron

The amount of heat used to bond the petals changes their color and can make them brittle. It is advisable to start with a low temperature—you can always increase the heat, but you can't revive a flower once it has been burned.

Purple bougainvillea petals were used in both the examples here. Petals were trapped in gray silk paper to match the trimming on the bag on the right. Little heat was applied when bonding the petals to the fabric so that the petals retained their original color.

The bougainvillea petals trapped on pulp paper in the bag below look very different. In order to achieve this rich mahogany color, the temperature of the iron was set on high. As a result, the petals changed color. The pulp paper and the petals, which densely covered the pulp paper, were painted with acrylic wax. Angelina fibers, skeleton leaves, and a sheer fabric were placed on top. The outlines of the skeleton leaves were stitched into. The panel was then appliquéd to the base fabric. Two panels were made so that the bag is reversible and there is no back or front.

The panel is robust once it is in position. When you make up the bag, ensure there is sufficient fabric surrounding it so that the bag can be sewn up with the right sides together, and it can therefore be turned inside out without destroying the pulp-paper panels on either side of the bag.

Bags incorporating bougainvillea petals.

Acrylic Paint, Crackle Varnish, Gold Interference, and Alcohol Inks

Using this technique achieves an end result that is waterproof and is still easy to stitch into. The paper takes on a plastic appearance and although that might sound unappealing, it is suitable for bag making because it becomes robust and scuff resistant. Any needle marks show once your needle pierces the paper, so you need to be sure that you are putting it in the right place. You could try painting on cocoon stripping paper, silk paper, and bought papers.

The clutch bag (right) was made from pulp paper that was dried over bubble wrap. Do not attempt to turn pulp paper inside out when you are making the bag. Sew the sides up with the insides together and paint the edges that show.

Method
1   Cover the pulp paper with a thick layer of acrylic paint.
2   When it is dry, apply a generous coat of crackle varnish.
3   When the varnish is almost dry but still quite tacky, apply a coat of gold interference acrylic paint.
4   Let this dry and then decide whether to leave it as it is or proceed with the next stage.

Using alcohol inks
Card makers use a variety of techniques to apply alcohol inks, but I find a dense make-up sponge and leftover strips of batting very effective for coloring large areas.

1   Protect your hands with rubber gloves and the work surface with plastic sheeting.
2   Pour blending solution onto the sponge.
3   Add two or three colors of ink and blending solution to the sponge and work it into the paper. It will take a little practice to see how much blending solution to add.

TIP: Alcohol inks work best on a shiny, nonporous surface. Using them on papers that haven't been treated doesn't work well. Also, using them on shiny card stock, as recommended for card makers, is not good as shiny cardstock is unsuitable for bag making.

Pulp paper dried over bubble wrap and colored with acrylic paint, crackle varnish, interference paint, and alcohol inks.

Clutch Bag Colored with Alcohol Inks

1   Make a solid sheet of cocoon stripping paper (see page 41).
2   Cut out a rectangle measuring 8½ x 16½ inches (22 x 42 cm).
3   Paint a layer of Ormoline mixed with water over the paper.
4   When this is dry, follow the instructions for using alcohol inks on the opposite page. Try out your chosen colors on a piece of scrap paper first to ensure suitability for your bag.
5   When the paper is dry, fold the bag in position and shape and cut the flap.
6   Open the paper out flat again and use it as a pattern for cutting the lining.

TIP: The edges of the lining will show as the bag will not be turned inside out so choose the lining carefully to ensure compatibility.

7   Bond the paper to the lining with 505 spray glue.
8   Attach magnetic fasteners.
9   Attach a brooch to cover the back of the magnetic fastener on the flap.
10 Handstitch or machine stitch the edges of the bag.

Cocoon stripping bag with an enameled badge.

Crackle Glaze Shoulder Bag

What to do

1   Cut the bag (a) and flap (b) patterns out of cotton rag paper. Shape the flap patterns.
2   Cut the lining larger to allow for turnings at the top.
3   Bond the paper to batting with 505 spray glue and cut the batting to size.
4   On scrap paper, using acrylic paint, crackle glaze and interference paint, experiment with colors to see which you prefer.
5   Apply your chosen colors to the bag patterns as described on page 66.
6   Add more color with alcohol inks.
7   With the feed dog down and using metallic thread, sew meandering horizontal lines across the bag. Sew vertical lines on the flap.
8   Put the insides together and sew up the seams.
9   Trim the edges if necessary and then use the same acrylic paint to color the edges.
10 Attach the magnetic fastener to the bag flap and the bag front. Alternatively, use Velcro.
11 Make the tassels or decoration of your choice and attach to the flap front.
12 Sew the two flaps together.
13 Sew the flap to the bag back.
14 Insert the handle of your choice. Decide whether to attach it to the outside or the inside. (For this bag I attached the handle to the outside, then covered it with velvet trim.)
15 Sew the edges of the lining with the right sides together.
16 Insert the lining and pull the top over the top edge of the paper.
17 Decide whether to use the lining as the top decorative border or whether to use the velvet trim. If you decide to use the velvet trim, it can be pinned and tacked in position.
18 Sew it in place.

TIP: Take your time considering this as all pin marks will show should you decide not to have a trim.

YOU WILL NEED:

- cotton rag paper: cut one piece 11 x 19¾ inches (28 x 50 cm) and two pieces 6¼ x 3¼ inches (16 x 8 cm)
- batting
- lining material
- 505 spray glue
- acrylic paint
- crackle glaze
- interference gold paint
- 3 alcohol inks
- metallic thread
- magnetic fastener or Velcro
- bag decoration for flap
- chain or cord handle
- velvet trim, 12 inches (30 cm) long and 1 inch (2 cm) wide

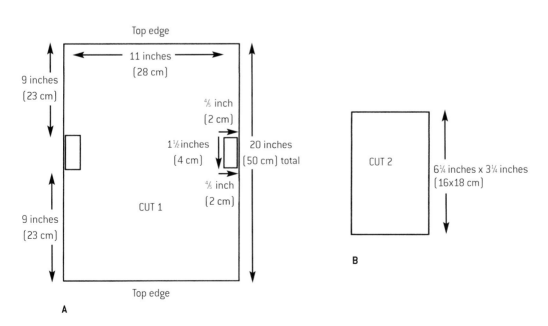

Machine Lace

This purse was made from colored sheers, pulp paper, and machine lace. The lace for this bag was made on a water-soluble fabric and then appliquéd to the pulp paper so that it "sat" on the top.

Aquatics Bond Stabilizer is fairly new on the market and is a very useful product. It is very easy to use and does not have to be stretched in a frame. The soluble fabric comes with a paper backing and it can be put through an ink-jet printer to reproduce your design. When the backing is peeled off one side is sticky. This can be adhered to silk paper as this can be washed and will therefore come to no harm when the Aquatics soluble fabric is dissolved. If you do this, your "lace" will be stitched onto the silk paper and will be an integral part of the design. In other words, it will sink into the paper rather than sitting on the top. Alternatively, ribbons, threads, and other materials that can be stitched into can be placed on the sticky side of the Aquatics fabric. Place a second sheet of soluble fabric over this, and the sandwich can be stitched into to make lace. When this is dissolved in water you are left with lace, which then has to be appliquéd to your base fabric.

Medieval-inspired bag.

Working with Bookbinder's Tissue

I have referred to this thin and rather fragile tissue as bookbinder's tissue throughout this book for consistency, but it is sometimes referred to as repair tissue, abaca tissue, or Tissutex. It can be bought in two weights, and I find that although the thinner tissue is more fragile, it is quite tactile and therefore makes an appealing bag. In order to use bookbinder's tissue for bag making it must be reinforced. I use wadding for this.

1   All the bags made from bookbinder's tissue have quilter's batting for the base. I have used 505 repositionable spray glue to adhere the tissue to the batting.
2   In addition to this, I frequently use a sheer silk scarf to go over the top of the colored tissue. These layers can either be stitched into as they are or the silk scarf can be bonded to the tissue with fusible webbing.

TIP: The webbing really needs to be colored if you choose this option.

3   Coloring the paper and then waxing it also makes it stronger. Acrylic wax can be painted on it or encaustic wax can be used to transfer pattern. This should be covered with a layer of acrylic wax or encaustic wax sealer.
4   To stitch into the sandwiched layers (batting, bookbinder's tissue, and sheer silk scarf), it is necessary to stretch the layers in an embroidery frame. Care therefore needs to be taken to ensure that the bag pattern fits your embroidery frame as needle and pin marks will show.

Wet-strength conservation tissue is stronger than bookbinder's tissue, but I do not find it as appealing for bag making. However, the bag (below) was made from wet-strength conservation tissue, stamped, and colored with Twinkling H_2O paints and protected by a coat of acrylic wax.

Bag made from wet-strength conservation tissue.

PROJECT

Teabag Paper and Diaper Liners

Much of my inspiration comes from medieval and Renaissance architecture and an interest in brass rubbing as a student. Nowadays brasses are revered, and it is not possible to take rubbings from the original source. There are, however, places where you can go to take rubbings of replicas.

Try taking parts of designs and play around with them on tracing paper and architect's design paper until you have come up with something that is your own. The brass depicting Margaret Peyton at Isleham in Cambridge, England, has yielded lots of designs for me. Playing around with the design on her dress produced the fabric opposite.

There is quite a lot of subtle texture in diaper liners and teabag paper. It is only when you paint on it that it becomes more obvious. Try placing one on top of the other—securing them so that they do not move—and paint on top.

YOU WILL NEED:
- diaper lining
- batting
- teabag paper
- gold bronzing powder
- Ormoline guilding medium
- gold embroidery thread
- pearl beads
- gold beads
- metal necklace for handle
- fastening (see step 11)

Medieval-inspired evening bag closed with purpose-made rings (see detail, above).

Method
1   Draw your design on tracing paper.
2   Place a diaper liner over the completed design on the tracing paper and secure with masking tape.
3   Use a gold pen to outline the design.
4   Now remove the masking tape.
5   Make a sandwich with three layers of fabric: quilter's batting, teabag paper, and diaper liner with the design.
6   Stitch all three layers together around the edges so that they do not move.
7   Add color in sections by painting a mixture of gold bronzing powder and Ormoline on the fabric. (Remember the safety precautions when working with bronzing powders.) The bronzing powder mixture may bleed into the teabag paper underneath.
8   Stretch the fabrics in a frame and use gold threads to embroider it.
9   Add pearl beads and gold beads.
10 Add a handle. This one was made from a metal necklace.
11 Add a fastening. This bag is fastened by pulling the gold elastic loop over the two rings, which are sewn to each side of the bag at the top. The rings were made from jewelry findings. Oven-dried clay disks were made to fit in them. They were decorated by triple embossing enamels with a stamp pressed in.

Pattern from Stamps

Stamps from heat blocks

There are so many wonderful ready-made stamps to be bought that it is easy to be seduced. However, making your own stamps is good fun, and you will end up with an original design. Reusable heat blocks are a good way to experiment. Simply heat the block with a heat tool and press it into a raised surface. Searching for interesting raised surfaces can prove to be an exciting adventure. Try heating the block and pressing it into some raised embroidery, such as crewelwork. It doesn't harm the embroidery, and if you don't like what you see, you can reheat the block and start again. Sometimes it is worth inking up the block on an ink pad and trying it out before you discard it, as surprising results can be achieved.

You could also try making your own raised surface on copper shim in which to press the heat block:

- Begin by drawing your design on tracing paper.
- Transfer the design to copper shim and emboss it.
- Use a heat tool to heat a foam block and press it into the embossed shim.
- Use the stamp with an ink pad.

Stamps from Funky Foam

1   Choose your design source, preferably one that is not copyrighted. Trace the image onto tracing paper.
2   Transfer the design onto the Funky Foam.
3   Cut it out with scissors or with a soldering iron. A soldering iron is particularly useful if the design is more intricate. Work in a well-ventilated room and wear a respirator and mask if you are using a soldering iron.
4   Marks can be made in the foam using a soldering iron to give more definition.
5   Use PVA glue to bond the Funky Foam image to a wooden block.
6   When the PVA is dry, the stamp is ready to use.

TIP: Keep the design simple. For Funky Foam, you may need to search Internet sources if not locally available.

The flower stamp used to decorate the bag (left) was made from Funky Foam.

Using Funky Foam and a heat block together
Using a heat block and Funky Foam together for the same design produces interesting results.

1   Make a stamp using Funky Foam as explained opposite. You can use the image you cut out and the remaining foam you cut it out from if you use a soldering iron. This way you will obtain two images.
2   Heat up a foam block and press it into a stamp. You will now have positive and negative images to work with.

The shoulder bag below was made from silk paper stamped with a primitive design. The stamp was made by using Funky Foam and a heat block together as described above.

Silk paper shoulder bag, stamped with a homemade stamp.

String block stamps and heat blocks

Printing blocks are easily and cheaply made using string on card stock or wooden blocks. A thistle block stamp made in this way was used to decorate the bag below.

1   Use a pencil to draw a simple design on a wooden block. (If you do not have a block, you can use thick card stock.)
2   Use PVA glue to bond string to the pencil outline. (This technique is rather messy! If you find this difficult, try sticking double-sided tape over the pencil drawing and attach the string to this.)
3   If you want to print with this design, paint PVA over the string to stop your printing medium soaking into it. When it is dry, you can print with the block.
4   Try heating a foam block and press it into the string block. You will then have a positive and negative image to work with.

The bag below was stamped into with a homemade stamp on bookbinder's tissue. Texture was added with fresco flakes, and the paper was protected with acrylic wax and varnish. The tag was made from textured silk paper and was embroidered in stumpwork.

Thistle bag with
stumpwork tag.

Stamps from Softsculpt (heat-moldable foam)

Softsculpt (sometimes called Formafoam; search Internet sources if not available locally) is another material that requires heat to gain an impression. When working with Softsculpt, you need to work very quickly and exert a lot of pressure. Look for unusual objects to press into the heated Softsculpt. A shell bracelet was used to make the Softsculpt impressed stamp for the bag below.

Try

- Making a stamp from heat-moldable foam.
- Stamp onto silk paper.
- Color the background with paints of your choice. (I used Twinkling H_2O paints here.)
- Add more color to the stamped area if necessary.
- Consider using encaustic wax on any raised areas. (I used brown encaustic wax here.)
- Use acrylic wax to protect it and make it waterproof.
- The Softsculpt impressed foam can also be incorporated in the design. Try not to include it if it appears to be "plonked on," but you could consider using it for a tab in some cases.
- Stitch into the silk before making it up into the bag pattern.

Bohemian bag made from silk paper.

Primitive clutch bag.

Primitive Clutch Bag

This bag has an aged appearance and the designs on it are reminiscent of primitive cave paintings or ancient Egyptian art. It is made from a base of store-bought paper artificially aged with coffee, shoe polish and dye, and decorated using a rubber stamp and embossing ink. Stamps can be either bought commercially or you can make your own.

Method

1   Cut the sheet of felt paper to a size of about 18 x 10 inches (45 x 25 cm), either by tearing it with your hands or using a soldering iron, which can give attractive-looking burned edges.
2   Color the paper using a sponge soaked in cold coffee and leave to dry.
3   Use the rubber stamp and ink pad to print the design onto the paper in a repeat pattern. Shake embossing powder over the design, tap off the excess, and apply the heat tool to emboss it.
4   Paint the shapes using Procion dye. Leave to dry. Procion and other fiber-reactive dyes must be sealed to be safe (A).
5   Iron the paper in between two sheets of baking parchment.
6   Embroider randomly around the shapes using straight stitches and the variegated metallic thread on your sewing machine.
7   Color the paper further by rubbing shoe polish gently into it, then buff it with a wax furniture polish (B).
8   Apply a coat of varnish to the paper and leave to dry.
9   Bond the paper to the curtain interlining using the spray glue and cut away any excess fabric, then use coffee to color the edges of the fabric.
10   Fold the bag into three sections to form an "envelope" shape and sew a strip of Velcro into place where the flap joins. Sew on a decorative brooch or bead at the center of the flap.
11   Using spray glue, bond the whole piece of fabric, interlining side down, to the suede-effect fabric. Cut away any excess fabric.
12   Stitch all around the fabric using a sewing machine or by hand, then fold the bag in position and sew up the sides.

YOU WILL NEED:

- 1 large sheet of felt-finish paper
- soldering iron (optional)
- coffee granules
- sponge
- rubber stamp
- black embossing ink pad and embossing powder
- paintbrushes
- brown Procion dye
- iron
- baking parchment
- variegated metallic sewing thread
- sewing machine (optional)
- brown shoe polish
- beeswax furniture polish
- varnish
- 505 spray glue
- 18 x 10 inches (45 x 25 cm) piece curtain interlining
- 4 inches (10 cm) strip Velcro
- brooch or bead for fastening
- 18 x 10 inches (45 x 25 cm) piece suede-effect fabric for lining

A

B

Waxes for Waterproofing and Color

The basic recipe I use for waterproofing comprises a coat of acrylic wax, followed by beeswax polish and finally either a clear glaze or clear nail polish. Ordinary varnish, although it is cheaper, can make the paper too brittle. Stitching tends to pull away from such brittle paper.

You do not always need to use a glaze. It all depends on the paper, the paint and the way in which you want to use it. I have used it on occasion to ensure a shiny surface to enable color to be added with alcohol inks.

Encaustic Wax over Raised Surfaces

The shopping bag on the left was made with a bought textured cotton rag paper.

1. Add texture and pattern by gluing on rectangles of cartridge or heavy drawing paper.
2. Paint brown Procion dye all over the paper.
3. When this is dry, heavy gloss gel, sand texture gel, and copper bronzing powder should be mixed on a plastic table mat and applied to the paper with a roller (brayer). Remember the safety precautions that accompany powders and dyes.
4. Colored encaustic wax is now applied by melting the wax on the iron and quickly moving it over the textured paper so that it only soaked into the raised areas. (If you do not have an encaustic iron a travel iron will do. A steam iron is unsuitable.)
5. Leave the wax in place. To give more shine the paper can be painted with acrylic wax.
6. Beeswax polish is then applied and rubbed in.
7. The paper is bonded to batting and threads couched down to emphasize the grid-like structure.
8. Now cut the pattern to size and make your bag. (Remember that these papers cannot be turned inside out.)
9. Add handles. The handles of this bag were made out of woven metal tubing.
10. The batting on the open seam can now be painted with brown Procion dye so that the seam is not too obvious.

Right: Cocoon stripping bag. Color was added with coffee and shoe polish with acrylic wax to seal it.

Left: Encaustic wax over raised surfaces.

PROJECT

Encaustic Wax Shopping Bag Made from Wallpaper

Method

1   Cut the wallpaper 20 x 11 inches (50 x 28 cm). Shape the wallpaper as shown in the bag diagram on page 69.
2   Color the textured wallpaper with the bronzing powder mixed with the acrylic wax. Wear a respirator and mask and work in a well-ventilated area. Use a paintbrush to apply the paint and push it into the crevices so that all the paper is covered.
3   When it is dry, melt the encaustic wax on a travel iron or encaustic iron and lightly iron it on the paper. It will color the raised areas and the gold paint will remain in the crevices.
4   Bond the paper to the batting with the spray glue. Trim the batting to size.
5   Manipulate the mulberry bark by soaking the fibers and pulling them into shape. You need the two strips to be quite dense.
6   Dye the paper dark brown. (I boiled the mulberry bark in ferrous sulphate to achieve this color.)
7   Create tiles from Mylar Sheetz, as follows:
  •   Place the Mylar on a spongy mouse pad.
  •   Heat the Mylar.
  •   Press a wooden stamp into the Mylar.
  •   Cut the tiles to size and color with alcohol inks.
8   Stitch into the Mylar.
9   Appliqué the tiles to the mulberry bark strip.
10 Sew around the outline in backstitch.
11 Center the strips on the painted wallpaper and sew them in place.
12 Fold the bag with right sides together and sew the edges.
13 Trim any excess fabric and paint the edges with acrylic blue paint.
14 Tear the handles out from a paper shopping bag and wrap them with knitting ribbon.
15 Trim any excess paper and use PVA glue to stick the handles in position.
16 Sew up the sides on the lining with the right sides together.
17 Fold the top edge over and insert it in the bag.
18 Pin the lining to the bag top. (Any pin marks will show, so it is best to put the pins on the sewing line.)
19 Sew the lining in place.

YOU WILL NEED:
• textured wallpaper
• scissors
• gold bronzing powder
• acrylic wax
• paintbrush
• encaustic iron or travel iron
• 20 x 11 inches (50 x 28 cm) batting
• 20 x 11 inches (50 x 28 cm) lining material
• green Mylar Sheetz
• wooden stamp
• 2 strips mulberry bark, 11 x 22 inches (5 x 55 cm)
• sewing machine
• alcohol inks
• embroidery threads
• blue encaustic wax
• paper handles from a shopping bag
• ribbon to wrap handles
• PVA glue
• acrylic blue paint
• 505 spray glue

Encaustic wax shopping bag.

Encaustic Wax Resist over Embossing Trays

If you use bookbinder's tissue for this technique, the resulting paper is reminiscent of silk. Plastic embossing trays sold for children to rub wax or colored pencils over a sheet of paper are very useful for this technique, but the wax will not wash out or melt out so if you want your trays to remain in pristine condition, don't use them for this technique (this is applicable to any raised surface you use).

Method
1   Rub colored encaustic wax over the raised surface on the tray.
2   Cut a sheet of bookbinder's tissue to the size of the tray, leaving a border of about 1 inch (2.5 cm) all around. (You may prefer to use lightweight bookbinder's tissue as it is more translucent and feels like working in silk, although it is fragile. The heavyweight version does not feel so appealing when it is made into a bag.)
3   Secure the tissue to the work surface and over the tray with masking tape.
4   Iron over the tray. The wax will be transferred to the paper. Experiment with the amount of wax needed. Load the flat surface of the iron with more wax if necessary.

TIP: Remove the paper from the tray or raised surface immediately as the wax will dry right away, and the paper will stick to the tray.

5   Leave the wax in the paper and paint in the spaces. I use Twinkling H_2O paints. The paper is porous, so it is best to paint it on baking parchment to prevent it from seeping through and sticking to any other surface.
6   Heat fixes the dyes if necessary. To do this, place baking parchment on the ironing board with newspapers to soak up any excess wax before ironing.
7   Apply a generous coat of acrylic wax. This protects the Twinkling H_2O paints and makes the paper more robust.
8   In an embroidery frame place a sandwiched layer of batting, the colored tissue, and a white sheer fabric. (The quality of the batting determines the feel of the fabric as does the sheer fabric. I prefer silk scarves.)
9   Embroider the fabrics.

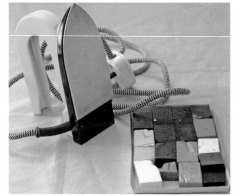

Encaustic iron and waxes.

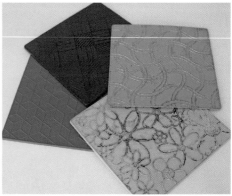

Plastic embossing trays.

Encaustic wax patterns
obtained from embossing
trays and on the raised areas
of pulp paper. All of the
samples colored with
Twinkling H20 paints.

PROJECT

Soft-feel Bags

An old frame was reused for this bag, which was made from bookbinder's tissue.

Method

1 Use an embossing tray to iron the pattern onto four pieces of tissue. (I used white encaustic wax.)
2 Color the areas that are not waxed. Consider which paints or dyes you use as these contribute to the feel of the bag (I used Procion dyes but silk dyes and Twinkling H_2O paints work well for a soft feel). Color the tissue on a sheet of baking parchment to eliminate the possibility of the tissue sticking to a surface and subsequently tearing.
3 For added protection, paint a coat of acrylic wax over the tissue. (I wanted to maintain a soft feel, so I did not do this.)
4 Use 505 spray glue to bond each of the four pieces of tissue to batting. (I used cotton batting as it is soft to the touch and drapes well.)
5 Place a sheer fabric over the tissue. (I used a white sheer silk scarf.)
6 Stretch the sandwiched layers in an embroidery frame.
7 Experiment with different threads and needles on scrap tissue bonded to batting to see which thread you prefer. (It is essential that you do this as needle marks will show if you decide to unpick a thread. Choose the correct needle for the thread so that you do not make too large a hole in the tissue. I used variegated cotton to accentuate the soft feel I wanted for this fabric.)
8 Stitch into the tissue with your chosen thread.
9 Bead the fabric if desired.
10 Sew the embroidered pieces of fabric together, add lining, and attach them to a frame.

YOU WILL NEED:
- embossing tray
- Procion dyes
- acrylic wax
- 505 spray glue
- batting
- sheer fabric
- variegated sewing thread
- beads (optional)
- bag frame
- lining fabric

Evening bag with a reused vintage frame.

Bookbinder's Tissue

This again is bookbinder's tissue with the pattern added by melting encaustic wax over an embossing tray. Four pieces of tissue were waxed and the waxed pattern was colored with silk dyes and embossing enamels. The fabric was bonded onto batting and a sheer scarf laid on top prior to stitching. The flowers were crudely machine embroidered and handstitched. After applying a coat of acrylic wax, the final layer of color was added using alcohol inks. Beads were stitched on for final decoration.

Enameled evening bag.

5 EVENWEAVE FABRIC AND APPLIQUÉ

Embroidery stitches that require an evenweave fabric in order to count the spaces can be worked successfully on papers. Cross-stitch, blackwork stitches, and canvaswork can all be worked on evenweave fabric from the back.

Tips for embroidering on paper

- If you want sharp, clean lines, thick papers are unsuitable for this technique as it is difficult to control the direction of the thread through thick layers.
- Experiment with your chosen threads on the evenweave fabric and paper before you begin. This sampler will enable you to ascertain the suitability of the thread on the evenweave and paper. Threads usually lie on the top and don't sink in. Some threads can look unappealing with this technique. Variegated machine embroidery thread works well for intensive stitching on bookbinder's tissue.
- Use repositionable glue like 505 to bond the paper to the evenweave fabric. This eliminates the time needed to tack the layers together and this glue doesn't prevent you from removing the evenweave threads from the back when you have finished.
- Use a pair of tweezers to remove the threads. It is easier to remove the threads if you begin by taking out all of the horizontal threads first.
- Sometimes the evenweave fabric can remain in place to give the bag the correct feel. However, the threads will probably need to be removed if you intend to appliqué your piece to another fabric.
- As you may be working through a number of layers, the fabrics must be stretched in an embroidery frame before you begin. It is advisable to consider the pattern size at this stage. Pin marks will show on the paper, so the frame should be large enough to accommodate the bag pattern. You may need to pin three sides of the paper to the frame and pin the evenweave only to the remaining side. When the embroidery on the stretched side is completed, the pins should be removed and the other side should be stretched in the same manner. This eliminates unsightly pin holes in the base of the bag.
- If at all possible, tab positions, seams, and magnetic fasteners should be considered if you are beading. (It's very frustrating to complete a lot of intensive handstitching and beading and then discover that you need to remove some of the beading.)
- A sheer fabric is often necessary to protect the paper as handbags need to be robust. Abaca tissue and bookbinder's tissue are both suitable for this technique but you must have a sheer fabric over it when you are embroidering.
- A blunt-end tapestry needle is not so good when working on bookbinder's tissue, silk paper, or any paper where the needle hole shows. A sharp needle with a narrow eye is preferable.
- Hold the needle in a vertical position to execute the stitch.
- Do not begin with a waste knot as there will be a hole left in the paper. An easy option is to secure the end on the back with masking tape and remove it later. The end can then be worked into the back of the stitches.

Silk paper background with degummed silk filament paper dragons and cocoon-stripping paper panel embroidered in blackwork.

Blackwork Merino Top Bag

Method

1   Draw your pattern pieces on to scrap paper and cut them out.
2   Stretch the evenweave fabric in an embroidery frame. Check that the pattern fits on it.
3   Cut the pattern pieces out in merino top paper.
4   Use 505 repositionable spray glue to bond the merino paper to the evenweave fabric.
5   Take the pins out of the frame and place the black sheer over the fabrics. Pin this sandwiched layer back on to the frame.
6   Make note of any obstructions, such as tab and Velcro positions and seams for when you are beading (mark these on the evenweave fabric if desired).
7   Use metallic machine embroidery thread to embroider your blackwork stitches.
8   Sew tiny beads on in appropriate places. Avoid beading seam, Velcro, and tab positions.
9   Remove the fabric from the frame and cut the pattern out, leaving a border of about $1\frac{1}{8}$ inches (3 cm) all round the sheer fabric.
10 Serge the edges.
11 Repeat this process with the other side of the bag and then, right sides together, sew the seams.

Making the tab

1   Cut the Softsculpt slightly smaller than the fabric for the tab. The fabric covering the tab will be turned in to enclose the Softsculpt.
2   Assemble layers of evenweave fabric, Softsculpt, merino top paper, and finally black sheer.
3   Embroider the blackwork pattern into these layers.
4   Bead the fabric, keeping away from the edges and the stitch line. This is the tab top.
5   Make the bottom of the tab by layering up the fabrics; evenweave, silk paper, and black sheer. Sew the smooth Velcro in position.
6   Embroider but do not bead this section.
7   Turn the edges in and slip-stitch them in place.
8   Put the back and front of the tab together and turn the edges in on the tab front.
9   Oversew the edges with the embroidery thread.
10 Stuff a length of tubular ribbon with the rug wool and make a long chain of single crochet with this. (It needs to fit round the tab.)
11 Sew this braid to the outside edges of the bag, starting at the back. Place the flat side down so that the raised, textured side is showing.
12 Bead round the outside of the tab, between the crochet chain stitches.
13 Tuck the ends of the ribbon in at the back. These will not show when you stitch it in place on the bag back.
14 Sew the tab to the back of the bag.
15 Sew a row of small beads on to cover the stitching. Sew a large bead in the center to make it a feature.

YOU WILL NEED:

- 2 sheets merino top paper, $9\frac{1}{2}$ x $9\frac{1}{2}$ inches (24 x 24 cm) each
- 2 pieces merino top paper, $3\frac{1}{2}$ x 7 inches (9 x 17 cm) for the tab
- 2 pieces lining material, $9\frac{1}{2}$ x $9\frac{1}{2}$ inches (24 x 24 cm)
- handles from paper shopping bag
- metallic variegated machine embroidery thread
- beads
- masking tape
- tubular knitting ribbon
- rug wool or thick wool to stuff the ribbon
- $1\frac{1}{8}$ inches (3 cm) Velcro
- evenweave fabric—sufficient to cover the silk paper pattern and fit in an embroidery frame
- PVA glue
- 505 spray glue
- black sheer fabric to cover the silk paper
- a thin sheet of Softsculpt for the tab
- large bead for the back of the bag (optional)
- embroidery frame

Blackwork merino top bag.

Detail of blackwork merino top evening bag on previous page.

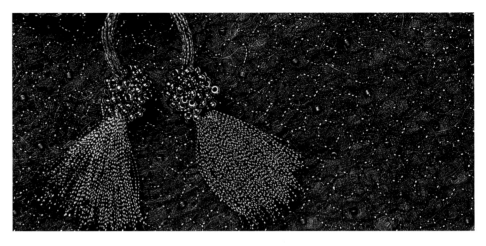

Making the tassles

1   Prepare a 3½ inch (9 cm) length of stuffed ribbon.
2   Take two pieces of cardstock, measuring 1½ x 1 inch (4 x 3 cm). Wrap the machine embroidery thread around the card about 100 times.
3   Thread the needle and insert it through the top of the card.
4   Tie the top to hold the threads in place. Hold on tight to the threads and the card at the top.
5   Cut the bottom ends of the threads by sliding the scissors through the two pieces of card.
6   Lift the card out, holding tightly on to the threads.
7   Open the tied strip out and wrap it around the stuffed ribbon.
8   Tie thread around the tassel so that the ribbon is inside.
9   Bead the bulbous part of the tassel.
10 Sew lots of beads on in a random fashion so that it becomes a chunky cluster. Stitch through the layers of thread and the stuffed ribbon so that it is all firmly anchored.
11 Do the same to the other end of the stuffed ribbon. Tie a knot in the ribbon and attach it to the center of the tab. Sew a cluster of beads just above the join.
12 Line the tab up with the bag front. Sew the remaining piece of hooked Velcro in position.
13 Stuff about 20 inch (50 cm) of tubular ribbon with the rug wool and sew it to the outside edge of the bag front.
14 Remove the paper handles from the shopping bag.
15 Trim the paper to fit the bag. Use masking tape to anchor one end of the variegated machine embroidery thread to the paper and wrap the thread round the handles. If it becomes necessary to join the thread, use double-sided sticky tape. Fit the handles in the bag. Measure the distance from the sides and mark the inside of the bag as a guide for sticking. Use PVA to stick the paper in position.

The lining

1   Cut out two pieces of lining material using your paper pattern. Sew around the edges, leaving the top open. Turn the top edge in on the bag by ¾ inch (2 cm). Slip-stitch it down. Iron the top of the lining in ¾ inch (2 cm) and then insert it in the bag.
2   Slip-stitch around the top. You can use invisible thread to sew the lining in or you can use the metallic thread. If desired, you can stuff the ribbon and sew this piping in the inside. This will make the inside look appealing when you open the bag.

Rayon Floss Paper

Keep the cut-off ends from rayon floss when you are embroidering with rayon. When you have sufficient ends, follow the instructions for making silk paper in the section on making paper from fibers (see page 27). Fluff out the rayon floss and treat it like silk fibers.

This bag (right) was made with rayon floss. The resulting paper was placed over red evenweave linen, stretched in an embroidery frame, embroidered in blackwork and beaded.

The handle was made from hollow plastic tubing with strips of red silk paper wound around it. It was further enhanced by wrapping the handle with the same thread used to embroider the paper. Wrap in one direction all the way round and then wrap in the other direction so that you get a criss-cross pattern. Beads were sewn on the handle to match those used on the fabric of the bag.

The buttons on the sides were crocheted with stuffed knitting ribbon.

The tassels were made from the same metallic machine embroidery thread used for the blackwork stitching.

Blackwork evening bag on rayon floss paper.

Woven canvas paper samples.

Paper Canvas Shopping Bag

This bag, made with purchased woven canvas paper, has been simply embroidered with canvaswork stitches.

Method

1   Sew the canvas paper to the curtain interlining around the outside edge and overlock the edges.
2   Fold the fabric in half and mark the center on the interlining.
3   Open the fabric out and draw a rectangle measuring 1½ x 3 inches (4 x 8 cm) on each side of the center line (see the diagram below).
4   Cut these two rectangles out and overlock the edges.
5   Embroider and bead the fabric.

Optional embellishment

•   Use a palette knife to spread the Paper Perfect pulp over the embroidered canvas, leaving some areas exposed. When it is dry, color the paper with a product such as Pébéo Setacolor fabric paints thinned with water or Procion dye.
•   Iron the bag with yellow and brown encaustic wax. The wax stays on the raised areas.
•   Olive green Procion dye can now be painted over the remaining areas.
•   The bag can finally be painted with varnish.

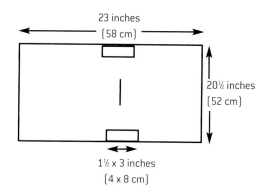

23 inches
(58 cm)

20½ inches
(52 cm)

1½ x 3 inches
(4 x 8 cm)

6   Put the right sides together and sew up the sides. Turn the bag the right side out.

7   Sew the side seams for the lining.

8   Plait the rope and sew the handles in position.

9   Cut the card to size and insert it in the bag.

10   Turn the top in ¾ inch (2 cm).

11   Insert the lining and turn the top in.

12   Slip-stitch the lining to the top.

13   Sew the rope piping to the top edge of the bag with invisible thread.

TIP: Woven canvas paper can be purchased by mail order from specialist dealers (see Suppliers on page 126).

The tag

1   Cut two pieces of handmade pulp paper to size.

2   Color it with with the same encaustic wax.

3   For the frog, color a piece of Translucent Liquid Sculpey paper with bottle green alcohol ink (see page 107).

4   Draw the outline with a black Gelly Roll pen.

5   Cut out the frog and sew it to one side of the prepared tag.

6   The two pieces of pulp paper can now be placed with the insides together and then sewn together on the sewing machine.

7   Use hole punch in the top center.

8   Attach the tag to the bag. Here a silver chain with a fastener was threaded through and attached to the bag handle.

YOU WILL NEED:

- 20½ x 23 inches (52 x 58 cm) woven canvas paper
- 20½ x 23 inches (52 x 58 cm) curtain interlining
- 20½ x 23 inches (52 x 58 cm) lining material
- 20½ x 23 inches (52 x 58 cm) thick card stock
- rope to plait for handles— finished length 32 inches (80 cm)
- rope for top trimming, 30 inches (76 cm)
- beads
- embroidery cotton
- invisible thread
- Paper Perfect pulp
- Procion dye
- encaustic wax
- varnish

Paper canvas shopping bag with Paper Perfect.

Canvaswork on Paper

Tips for working with pulp paper

- Color the evenweave canvas if it is going to be seen.
- Pulp papers are not pliable, so they are best used for panels or in bags where the seams show. Pulp paper bags are difficult to turn inside out. If you do intend to sew the seams with the right sides together and then turn the bag inside out, you will need to leave a large border round the pulp paper panels to enable you to do this.
- Wherever possible, make more paper than you need and use the leftover paper to experiment with different embroidery threads and canvases. Use the best examples in your work but keep all your samples for future reference. These could perhaps be made into tags.
- A needle hole in the wrong place will show in pulp paper. Take care as you will be working from the back.
- For extra protection, place a sheer fabric over the pulp paper before embroidering into it. Silk scarves are invariably the best.
- Experiment with paint finishes. Try adding a layer of Paper Perfect to give it added strength. Or try painting a layer of acrylic wax or varnish over the colored paper to protect it.

This bag, called *Summer Fades Away*, was made using merino tops on mosquito netting.

Two Little Dicky Birds **Bag**

The pulp paper panel for the bag opposite was embedded in a crocheted frame.

Method

1   Stretch evenweave canvas in an embroidery frame.
2   Bond the colored pulp paper to the canvas with 505 repositionable spray glue.
3   Embroider decoration—in this case, medieval-style birds—from the back.
4   Remove the evenweave threads of the canvas with tweezers.
5   Appliqué the panel to the base fabric—a purchased metal-weave fabric.
6   Add embellishment as desired. Here French knots were worked in knitting ribbon, and stone beads were sewn in places.
7   The birds fly off the wall on the Softsculpt impressed zipper pull.
8   Attach a handle. This one was made from shoelaces bound with imitation leather piping. They were sewn to the bag, and the ends of the shoelaces were frayed. Stone beads were sewn around the bases.
9   Stitch the seams. The seams of this bag were sewn with the right sides together as there was sufficient room to turn the bag the right way out.

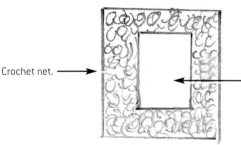

Crochet net.

Pulp paper in the open area and overlapping onto the crocheted frame.

This bag, entitled *Two Little Dicky Birds*, was made using a crocheted frame and pulp paper.

PROJECT

White Rubber Canvas and Merino Tops

TIP: As the canvas is rubber, the paint cannot be heat-fixed. With this in mind, select threads and ribbons that will complement a faded or chipped appearance. A nonfray lining is also advisable as this makes it easier to obtain a neat edge.

Method

1   Cut out two 2 x 3 inches (8 x 5 cm) rectangles. These are positioned on the center line as shown in the diagram, below.
2   Position the handles and draw the semicircular shapes on either side on the felt. This will enable you to ascertain where the handles will go so that you do not waste paint or threads in these areas. Do not cut out these semicircles at this stage, as it would be difficult to stretch the fabrics in an embroidery frame.
3   Paint the canvas.
4   When the canvas is dry, make sandwiched layers of felt, canvas, and merino tops paper. Stretch these in an embroidery frame. If you do not have a frame large enough, stretch one-half of the bag only as shown in the diagram but do not puncture the canvas.
5   Use thick threads and knitting or embroidery ribbons to embroider the fabrics using the canvas as an evenweave backdrop.
6   Bead the fabric.
7   Remove the fabric from the frame.
8   Pin the other side of the fabric to the frame and embroider and bead this side.
9   Check the position of the handles again and cut out the two semicircles.
10 Place the right sides together and sew the seams. Turn the bag right side out.
11 Wrap the handles with ribbon. Use double-sided tape to secure the ends.
12 Sew the seams on the lining and insert it in the bag.
13 Sew the lining to the bag around the top edges using the same ribbon and attach beads.
14 Use ribbon to attach the handles to the bag and the lining.

YOU WILL NEED:

- white rubber canvas, 18 x 14 inches (46 x 36 cm)
- merino top paper, 18 x 14 inches (46 x 36 cm)
- felt, 18 x 14 inches (46 x 36 cm)
- Stewart Gill Byzantia paint
- paintbrush
- ribbons and threads for embroidery
- beads
- 2 circular handles
- double-sided tape
- lining, 18 x 14 inches (46 x 36 cm)

Opposite: Bag made from white rubber canvas and merino tops.

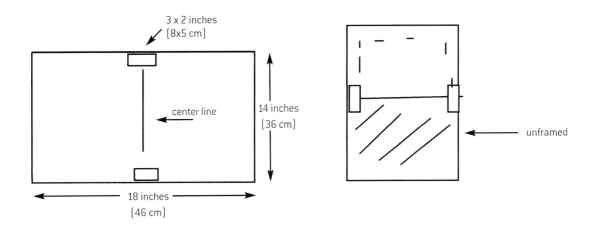

3 x 2 inches (8x5 cm)

center line

14 inches (36 cm)

18 inches (46 cm)

unframed

PROJECT

Square-based Bags

These bags, with a square base, open out into a square, boxy shape. They are fastened by tying the cords, which go through the wrapped washers that are sewn to the sides at the top of the bag. Cut out a pattern piece in paper as illustrated in the diagram below.

YOU WILL NEED:

- fabric
- lining fabric
- interlining
- 505 spray glue
- embroidery threads
- decorative fabric or appliqué shapes
- sewing thread
- Softsculpt shape or button
- cord
- washers
- invisible thread

Opposite: This Celtic pattern from a Dover publication is made from degummed silk filament paper. It was colored with bronzing powder mixed with acrylic wax. Patination fluid was used sparingly. (Remember the safety precautions.) The motif was appliquéd to dyed, hand-woven linen. The motif was cut out again and appliquéd to the store-bought fabric used to make the bag.

Method

1   Cut out four pattern pieces in the fabric of your choice.
2   Cut out four pattern pieces in lining material.
3   Cut out four pattern pieces in felt-feel curtain interlining.
4   Use 505 spray glue to adhere the curtain interlining to the fabric.
5   Embroider the fabric or appliqué shapes to the back and front.
6   Take the front and one side and put the right sides together. Starting at the point of the triangular base, sew down one side.
7   Take the back piece and put the right sides together with the remaining side of the side piece. Starting at the triangular base, sew up this seam.
8   Take the remaining side piece and put the right sides together with the back piece and sew up this seam.
9   Turn the bag in so that the final seam to be sewn has the right sides together. Sew in this seam.
10 Turn the bag right side out.
11 Turn the top edge in ¾ inch (2 cm) and slip-stitch it in position.
12 Take an appropriate Softsculpt shape or a button and sew it to the center on the base of the bag to cover the center join.
13 Make the lining up the same way and turn the top edge in.
14 Make the handles next. Attach them to the bag.
15 If you want the bag to retain its square base, cut out a piece of card measuring 5 x 5 inches (12 x 12 cm) and insert it into the base before sewing the lining in. (Trim the card stock if necessary.)
16 Insert the lining into the bag and slip-stitch it in place using invisible thread.
17 Wrap the washers or work buttonhole stitch around them.
18 Stitch the washers in position at the top of the bag.
19 Make a cord or a strap to thread through the washers.

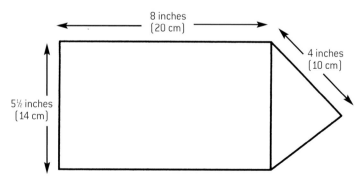

Alhambra Square-based Bag

The pattern for this bag, inspired by the
Alhambra Palace, is on the previous page.

What to do

1   Cut the bag sides from blue slub silk fabric
    and the front and back from silk paper.
2   Decorate the bag. The motifs on the front
    and back are silk paper, made from de-
    gummed silk filament. They were
    worked separately over a sandwiched
    layer of evenweave fabric, de-
    gummed silk filament paper,
    Angelina fibers, and a blue sheer
    fabric.
3   Add embroidery. Here, blackwork
    stitches were worked through the
    layers. When completed, they were
    cut out, and the woven threads
    from the evenweave were removed
    from the back by extracting them
    one at a time with tweezers.
4   The tops of the domes were
    painted gold and then the motifs
    were appliquéd to the back and
    the front panels of silk paper
    before they were beaded.
5   Softsculpt shapes disguise the
    base of the wrapped plastic
    handles. Use the same
    Softsculpt shapes at the ends of
    the cord. The gold paint used on
    the bag was gold bronzing
    powder, mixed with Ormoline.
    (Remember the safety
    precautions.) This paint will
    wear away when it is used on
    Softsculpt. However, if you
    want a distressed appearance
    this is great.

Square-based Bag in Bookbinder's Tissue

The thin bookbinder's tissue (sometimes called abaca tissue) used for this bag is more fragile than the heavier-weight version but it is the most appealing. You will need to cover the tissue with a silk scarf and stitch into it intensely to make a strong fabric.

What to do

1   Color the tissue. (Or buy it colored.)
2   Use an evenweave fabric in a matching or toning color. Bond the colored tissue to the evenweave fabric with 505 repositionable glue.
3   Cover the tissue with a colored silk scarf.
4   Stretch the layers of fabrics in an embroidery frame.
5   Use machine embroidery thread to embroider in blackwork stitches. These will have to be worked from the back.
6   Bead the fabric.
7   The handles used for this bag were made from brown paper shopping bag handles. They were wrapped with the same ribbon used for the trim.
8   The motif in the center of the tab is embossed copper shim.
9   Stuffed knitting ribbon was crocheted to go round the tab. The same ribbon was stuffed, and the wool used to stuff it was pulled tight to ruffle the ribbon. This was used to decorate the seams.

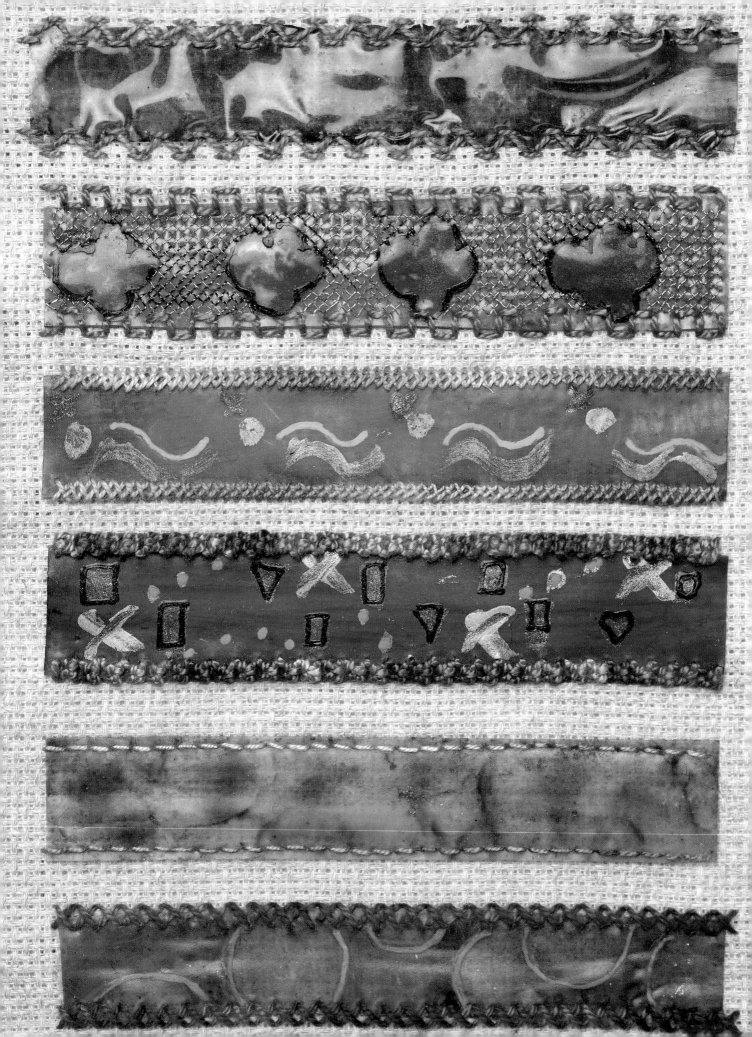

6 PAPER MADE FROM LIQUID CLAY

The translucent paper made from polymer liquid clay can be stitched into and colored and it is both challenging and rewarding to work with. It requires different techniques from making stand-alone transfers. As with all crafts, it takes a little practice. I have used both Kato polymer liquid clay and Translucent Liquid Sculpey (TLS). These products are sold primarily for transfer techniques. I found that the TLS was the most rewarding for bag making as it is easy to stitch into and is versatile.

Kato and Sculpey come in liquid form in bottles and require heat from an oven to set them. The oven temperature is crucial as it burns quite easily. It is advisable to take notice of the manufacturer's instructions and to keep an eye on it as ovens can vary. There will be an odor while the clay is cooking, but this is not toxic. The liquid clay is baked on a sheet of glass and is removed by cutting the edges away with a craft knife. It peels off easily, but if you only make one layer, you run the risk of it tearing as you lift it off.

Colors and images can be trapped between the layers and then baked to make them permanent. Alcohol inks, Gelly Roll pens, Permapaque markers, and Stazon ink pads all work well. Metal flakes, petals, flowers, and silk paper can be trapped between the baked layers and subsequently stitched into. Embossing powders, however, disintegrate if you stitch into them.

Method

1   Use a flat paintbrush that you keep for applying liquid clay. When not in use, store it in a plastic bag. Clean up with paper towels or baby wipes.
2   Paint the liquid clay onto a sheet of glass. I used glass from old photograph frames. (Make sure that the edges are not sharp.) Make sure the glass fits in the oven. Work out whether you want to make paper for motifs or bags so that you can select the appropriate size of glass for your project.

•   TLS will be quite cloudy when painted on the glass. (You can buy a solution called Diluent to dilute the liquid if it seems too thick. TLS does thicken over time but if it is new, the Diluent should not be necessary.) When the TLS is baked the front will be glossy and the back matt. This is an attractive quality that gives you the option to choose your required finish.
•   Kato clay spreads easily and is not so cloudy. When baked, both sides are glossy, and it can be made to resemble porcelain. Kato is more difficult to work with than TLS if you are stitching into it, as it has a tendency to split.
•   One layer of liquid clay is sometimes too thin to be used in areas requiring a robust fabric, so it is often better to bake two or three layers. Three layers can be quite difficult to stitch into, however. You have to get the balance right. Each layer should be thin.
•   Use baby wipes to clean up any smudges you make on the TLS paper when using Gelly Roll pens or similar.
•   When using Permapaque markers, use your finger to smudge the color. This must be done immediately before it has time to dry.
•   Blending fluid, which is made for use with alcohol inks, blends the colors and makes them paler as well.

The samples opposite were made with one layer of liquid clay. From top to bottom:
1. Colored with Tim Holtz denim and terra cotta alcohol ink.
2. Colored with terra cotta alcohol ink. Motifs outlined with a Gelly Roll pen with Stewart Gill Byzantia Excelsius paint in the center of the motifs (note that this flakes off so it is only acceptable for distressing).
3. Colored with a Permapaque marker on the background and Gelly Roll pens.
4. Colored with a Permapaque marker and Gelly Roll pens.
5. Colored with Tim Holtz wild plum and bottle alcohol inks (with blending fluid to dilute).
6. Colored with Tim Holtz wild plum alcohol ink and a Gelly Roll pen.

Using Alcohol Inks

These inks are the easiest way in which to apply color to translucent papers. For a sponged effect, dab the color on with a sponge or a piece of batting. For overall color, slide the inked sponge or batting over the paper. The addition of blending fluid blends the colors but also makes them paler. The color should be applied to the back of the paper as it will show through and will also be protected. It is not necessary to bake the color in order to set it.

Using Gelly Roll Pens

If you wish to use gel pens to color the paper, then you will find that Gelly Roll pens work the best. They should be heat-fixed to set them. This is best done in the oven.

Method

1   Paint a layer of Translucent Liquid Sculpey (TLS) on a sheet of glass.
2   Bake at 275°F (130°C) for 10 minutes.
3   Allow the glass and TLS to cool.
4   Draw with the Gelly Roll pen.
5   Bake in the oven for 10 minutes.
6   Color the TLS with alcohol inks or Permapaque markers.
7   Paint another layer of TLS on top.
8   Bake for another 10 minutes.
9   Remove the TLS from the glass by lifting one corner with a scalpel and pulling in one slow movement.

These purses were made from one layer of TLS. Because of the intensive stitching on the Nasturtium flower bag it remains strong enough for the purpose. It was colored with terra cotta alcohol ink and gold and black Gelly Roll pens.

The purple purse opposite was stamped with a purchased rubber stamp and baked prior to being colored with alcohol inks. A gold Gelly Roll pen was used to color in the outline on the design. The outline was then embroidered by hand in backstitch. Although the bag is soft and appealing to the touch, I would recommend using two layers of TLS to eliminate any threats of tearing or splitting (see page 107).

The bag below was also made from one layer. It was backed onto Softsculpt and would have benefited from being made from two layers of TLS. Stitch and Tear on top of the paper was necessary to facilitate the machine embroidery.

TLS bag with a wrapped ring handle and an enameled, stamped brooch.

PROJECT

Ca d'Oro Palace-inspired Paper Clay Bags

The bag below was made from one piece of TLS paper made on a large sheet of glass (remember to reverse the pattern for the other side of the bag when you are printing). The bag was made with the insides together so that it did not need to be turned inside out.

Porcelain-effect Kato clay bags

1 Set the oven to 275°F (130°C).
2 Paint one thin layer of Kato clay on the sheet of glass.
3 Bake for 10 to 15 minutes until the clay is set and leave it to cool.
4 Use a Stazon ink pad to ink up a stamp. Wear rubber gloves to do this. (If you have made your stamp as I did, it may be a good idea to bond it to a piece of wood with PVA glue.)
5 Bake the stamped clay again for 10 to 15 minutes to set the Stazon then leave to cool.
6 Paint another layer of liquid on to the first sheet and bake this for 10 to 15 minutes.

Ca d'Oro paper clay bag.

7   When it is cool, paint the third layer of liquid clay on and bake it again for 10 to 15 minutes.
8   The paper can now be embroidered. I found it was best to back it onto batting. Stretch the
     batting in a frame and place the paper clay over it.

Trapping beads and embroidery

1   Bake the first layer of clay as described above.
2   Use Stazon ink and a stamp to transfer your image to the paper on the glass.
3   Bake the paper to set the ink.
4   Remove the paper from the glass and place it over batting.
5   Embroider and bead the paper over the batting.
6   Place the batting and the embroidered paper back on the sheet of glass and paint a second
     layer of liquid clay over it.
7   Bake in the oven.

The embroidery and the beads will be
trapped between the two layers of
paper clay as in the bag below.

Ca d'Oro tower-block bag.
The face on the tag was
transferred to silk paper
with Image Maker.

7 TRANSFERRING IMAGES

When you are transferring images remember not to infringe copyrights. There are a lot of materials available for these techniques and most of them give a plasticized appearance and texture, which is very useful for shopping bags. Making your own shopping bag in these eco-aware times helps save wastage of plastic carriers and using photographs to personalize bags is popular.

Lady of Shalott Bag Using ExtravOrganza

ExtravOrganza is a semitransparent silk sheet with a paper backing. Images can be obtained by either printing using an ink-jet printer or by stamping. I had fun making this bag, partly because I was able to incorporate the priory from my hometown. All of the images on this bag were either printed in blue using an ink-jet printer or stamped in blue Stazon ink.

Method
1   Transfer your images. Here, drawings of the priory and of the lady at the well were isolated and printed onto the ExtravOrganza in blue. The backing paper was then removed.
2   Verses from the poem "The Lady of Shalott" by Alfred Tennyson were printed onto ExtravOrganza. The backing paper was then removed.
3   Stamp if desired. I used stamps to represent "the space of flowers" and Sir Lancelot. The flower stamp was made from four inkable Style Stones with a heat block pressed into them (the same style stones can then be painted and used as tags). The "space of flowers" stamp and the Sir Lancelot stamp was stamped over the printed verses.
4   Here, silk paper had texture added with Paper Perfect in the top area only. The paper was painted with Stewart Gill Byzantia paint and when it was dry, it was ironed to fix it.
5   Cut out your ExtravOrganza pieces and assemble on blue silk paper.
6   Stitch into the pieces and assemble the bag.

Knight stamp on printed ExtravOrganza (right) and Style Stone stamp (far right).

Lady of Shalott bag.

Girl with a Vase Bag

Image Maker by Dylon is not a new product, and it works very well on silk paper. If you can't find it locally, search eBay or websites that ship worldwide.

What to do

1. I began by making white silk paper. I cut three pieces to size and ironed them.

2. For the background, I used an embroidered piece I had made earlier. Handwoven fabric with silk paper incorporated had been embroidered to represent a Victorian garden wall. This was photographed and the image was printed in gray scale onto computer paper. Once you have your print, follow the manufacturer's instructions to spread Image Maker gel liberally over the front of the image. Place face down on the silk paper and leave to dry. Later, rub away paper backing with a wet paper towel. As it had been printed in gray scale, my resulting transfer was a pale version of the original.

3. The black-and-white drawing of the girl with the vase was photographed and printed in black and white on computer paper. Again, take your second image and spread Image Maker liberally over the top. Place face down on the second piece of prepared silk paper. When the paste is dry the paper backing can be removed with a wet paper towel. Cut out ready to assemble at a later date.

4. I painted a third piece of silk paper with gesso. This paper had a little more texture than the others, so I did not push the gesso into the crevices. Chroma Coal color pastels were blended and heat-fixed on this third sheet.

5. Cut gray suede fabric for the bag to size and bond to batting with 505 repositionable glue.

6. Position your silk pieces. Here, the three pieces of silk paper were placed in position, and the girl and vase were outlined in backstitch.

7. The border was made from embossed copper shim, and black acrylic paint was painted and quickly removed with a paper towel so that it only remained in the crevices. Color was added with alcohol inks. Sew your border in place with straight stitch on the sewing machine.

8. Four corner plates were made from Mylar Shimmer Sheetz and colored with alcohol inks. Sew these in place, and attach a wrought-metal bead in the center of each one. These decorative plates strengthened the corners to reduce the possibility of damage to the shim.

Uffizi Shopping Bag

I call this my Uffizi shopping bag because it was inspired by Italy, and I'm hoping it might persuade my husband to take me back there! And, yes, I know the face in the window isn't beautiful. I wanted an air of mystery (the reverse side can be seen on page 88).

What to do

1   The face at the window in the tower is a color photocopy that has been transferred onto silk paper using Image Maker as described on the previous page. Remember that the paper onto which you are transferring the image should be white. If it isn't, then it should be painted with gesso first.

2   The tower is made from silk paper that has been colored in places with Goldfinger antiquing gel. It was embroidered in gold thread in blackwork stitches.

3   The two dragons at either side are made from red degummed silk filament paper, and the bag itself is made from green degummed silk filament paper. The dragons were aged by painting gold bronzing powder mixed with Ormoline on them. Parts of them were painted with patination fluid while the bronzing powder was still wet, as patination fluid does not work on dry paint. Use it sparingly as it does not show up immediately. Remember the safety precautions when working with bronzing powders and patination fluid. Over time, gold bronzing paint loses its vibrancy and becomes muted. This is great if you want an aged effect, as I did.

4   The Uffizi bag is closed by a magnetic fastener. It also has a decorative fastener made from Mylar Shimmer Sheetz, which was heated with a heat tool and pressed into a pierced decorative silver spoon. The Mylar sheet was colored with alcohol inks to tone with the bag. A glass bead was sewn in the middle. The loop on the other side of the bag pulls over the Mylar-sheet brooch.

Left: Front of the bag with
Mylar brooch fastening and
Image Maker face on silk
paper.

Below: Detail of the window on
the reverse side of the Uffizi
bag (see also on page 88).

Yorkshire Dales Shoulder Bag

This bag was made using Dylon Image Maker and ink-jet transfer paper, which is great for transferring landscapes to silk paper. Holiday snaps and photographs of favorite places all work with this technique. The image on this bag is an embroidered scene representing the Yorkshire Dales. The shadow-work embroidery was photographed and printed onto the ink-jet transfer paper.

YOU WILL NEED:

- silk paper
- Dylon Image Maker
- Dylon transfer paper
- white gesso
- permanent markers
- encaustic wax
- acrylic wax
- beeswax polish
- 505 spray glue
- lining fabric
- magnetic fastener
- curtain weight

Method

1 Cut silk paper to your pattern size.
2 Prepare your image and print it onto a sheet of ink-jet transfer paper.
3 Use white gesso to paint the area where you want to transfer your design.
4 When the gesso is dry, iron the image onto the fabric following to the manufacturer's instructions.
5 Peel off the paper backing.
6 Add color if necessary with permanent marker pens.
7 This bag was given more texture by ironing encaustic wax over the green silk paper above and below the transfer. This gives it an aged effect.
8 Use a coat of acrylic wax and beeswax polish to waterproof the fabric. I also added encaustic wax sealer. This gives a nice weathered effect and tones with the printed Dylon image (note how this paper now differs from that used on page 117).
9 Bond the silk paper onto batting and stitch into it—I used 505 repositionable glue as it is easy to stitch into.

This bag is fastened with a magnetic fastener. The handles that make it into a shoulder bag are made from the weights that are sold in curtain boutiques to make sheer curtains hang straight. The fabric around the weights was dyed to match the bag.

The bird tag was made on card stock. Triple embossing enamels were melted, and a wooden stamp was pressed in after the stamp had been dusted with talcum powder to prevent it from sticking.

Yorkshire dales shoulder bag (opposite) and detail of the design (right).

119

TLS Stand-alone Transfers Using an Iron

Using Translucent Liquid Sculpey (TLS) is a very effective method of obtaining transfers. You must use black-and-white photocopies and not inkjet images for this method. A hard surface, but not an ironing board, is necessary for the ironing process—I use a wooden board.

Method

1   Cut out the image leaving a tab to aid the pulling-off process.
2   Cover the hard ironing surface with a sheet of baking parchment or baking Teflon.
3   Place the image front side up on the nonstick surface.
4   Pour a pool of TLS onto the front of the image and use your finger to spread the liquid. Try to keep your finger on the image so that no air can get trapped and do not cover the tab.
5   Cover the wet TLS with another sheet of baking parchment.
6   Heat the iron to the hottest setting (no steam) and lay it gently on the parchment. (Do not exert any pressure or move the iron about at this stage.)
7   After a few seconds the TLS should be set enough to allow you to exert pressure on the iron and carefully move it over the image.
8   After a few more seconds the transfer should be ready. Peel the baking parchment back a little. If it lifts off without sticking, then it is done. The paper backing should be removed immediately. Hold the tab and pull the paper off in one movement.
9   The resulting transfers can be colored with permanent markers or alcohol inks, and they can be stitched into. Sheer fabrics can be placed over the TLS prior to ironing. Experiment with this to see the effects.

Silk paper bag with a TLS transfer border.

The appliquéd panel on this bag is made from pulp paper, which has fibers embedded into it. The girl on the beach is made from a stand-alone TLS transfer. ExtravOrganza was used to print the verse in the sea and a purchased stamp was used on ExtravOrganza for the sailing boat tag. The tag itself is made from silk paper with fresco flakes added for texture.

Family Bag

The faces on this bag were made from a black-and-white photocopy. Transfers were made using TLS. (As it was an old photograph I was working from, I wanted the images to look old and so a gray sheer silk scarf was placed over the liquid TLS prior to ironing.)

The clothes were embroidered in blackwork stitches on silk paper with an evenweave fabric behind. The evenweave threads were removed with tweezers. The silk paper and the three transfers were sewn to the embossed copper shim background. (The embossed copper had been colored with black acrylic paint, which was rubbed off quickly so that it only remained in the crevices. The final layer of color was added with alcohol inks.) The imitation leather commercial fabric for the bag was cut to size and the copper, silk paper, and the stand-alone TLS transfers were appliquéd onto it. To complete the aging process, a black sheer silk scarf was placed over the images of the girls. It was sewn in place and the edges were burned with a soldering iron to prevent them from fraying any further.

The TLS transfer (below) was also covered with a sheer scarf prior to ironing the liquid TLS. The black-and-white drawing looked a bit stark on black fabric. As it appeared to me to be a bit funereal, I decided to color it with two shades of alcohol ink.

TIPS:
- I found that one shade works well if you want to retain all of the details in the drawing. Two shades obliterated most of the details but gives a pleasing variation of color.
- Stitch sparingly into the transfer, otherwise the stitching acts like a cutting tool.
- Handstitch the transfer before you apply it to the base fabric.
- If you machine stitch, you will need to use Stitch and Tear.

TLS transfer border prior to
coloring and stitching.

Black-and-white Photocopies

Black-and-white photocopies can be transferred to silk paper by ironing the image face down on the paper. The photocopy should be new, and the silk should be smooth in order to achieve the best results. You can also use stand-alone transfers to combine with this technique (see page 120 for further instructions).

Eucalyptus Bag

A black-and-white drawing of a branch of eucalyptus was used to decorate this bag. The photocopied image was transferred to the silk paper by ironing. A stand-alone transfer using a photocopied section of the branch and TLS was colored with Permapaque markers and gel pens. It was placed in position on the silk paper, and the rest of the branch was colored using the same pens. The paper was bonded to batting prior to stitching.

Part of the series based on the Lady of Shalott (see page 112). The store-bought cotton rag paper was painted and embossed with distress powders. The castle is in silk paper. The windows are TLS. The Lady of Shalott was transferred to silk paper using Image Maker gel. Sir Lancelot's image was stamped onto computer linen paper.

Suppliers

For materials used in this book, go to craft suppliers and notions departments of fabric stores. Brands and products that are more common in the United Kingdom. often can be ordered online from websites with worldwide shipping or found on eBay or www.shop.com.

American Art Clay Co.
Brent Pottery Equipment
Genesis Artist Colors International
6060 Guion Road
Indianapolis, IN 46254-1222
(800) 374-1600
www.amaco.com
(Art and hobby supplies, metal sheets, shim)

After Midnight Art Stamps
PO Box 830
Laveen, AZ 85339-0763
(866) 634-9408
www.amstamps.com
(Opals Embossing Enamels, paper and stamping supplies)

Carriage House Paper
79 Guernsey Street
Brooklyn, NY 11222
(800) 669-8781
www.carriagehousepaper.com
(Papermaking supplies)

Clearsnap Inc.
PO Box 98
Anacortes, WA 98221
(888) 448-4862
www.clearsnap.com
(Stamping and paper supplies)

Craftynotions
www.craftynotions.com
(U.K. source for online orders of Opalettes embossing enamel powders, Translucent Liquid Sculpey, Paper Perfect, Mylar Shimmer Sheetz, sinamay, Tangle Tuff, Twinkling H_2O paints)

Crystal Palace Yarns
160 23rd Street
Richmond, CA 94804
(510) 237-9988
www.straw.com
(Bag handles)

Dick Blick Art Materials
PO Box 1267
Galesburg, IL 61402-1267
(800) 933-2542
www.dickblick.com
(ExtravOrganza and other art supplies)

Embroidery Adventures
PO Box 40504
Bellevue, WA 98015
(866) 270-9390
www.embroideryadventures.com or store.embroideryadventures.com
(Embroidery, metallics, and surface design supplies)

Fabrics to Dye For
PO Box 20
Bradford, RI 02808
(888) 322-1319
www.fabricstodyefor.com
(Sewing, quilting and surface design supplies)

Golden Artist Colors
188 Bell Road
New Berlin, NY 13411-9527
(800) 959-6543
www.goldenpaints.com
(Paint, mediums, additives, varnishes)

Impress Me
17116 Escalon Drive
Encino, CA 91436-4030
(818) 788-6730
www.impressmenow.com
(Stamping supplies, Impress Me stamps by Sherrill Kahn)

The Kunin Group
PO Box 5000
Hampton, NH 03843-5000
(800) 292-7900
www.kuninfelt.com
(Felt and craft supplies)

Meinke Toy
PMB#411, 55 E. Long Lake Road
Troy, MI 48085
www.meinketoy.com
(Softsculpt, silk carrier rods and U.K. surface design products)

MisterArt.com
913 Willard Street
Houston, TX 77006
(800) 721-3191
www.misterart.com
(ExtravOrganza)

Paper Direct
PO Box 35750
Colorado Springs, CO 80935-3570
(800) 272-7377
www.paperdirect.com
(color foil, papers)

Paverpol USA
35 Elmont Avenue
Baltimore, MD 21206
(877) 661-1559
www.paverpolusa.com
(Fabric hardeners, pigments, varnishes, fabric)

Pipedreamink
www.pipedreamink.com
(Website that lists retailers for Opals Embossing Enamels)

Polyform Products
1901 Estes Avenue
Elk Grove Village, IL 60007
www.sculpey.com
(Sculpey, Translucent Liquid Sculpey, and polymer clays)

Polymer Clay Express at TheArtWay Store
9890 Main Street
Damascus, MD 20872
(800) 844-0138
www.polymerclayexpress.com
(Art and hobby supplies)

www.quiltingarts.com
(Online store; surface design supplies, vanishing muslin)

Soft Expressions
1230 North Jefferson Street, Suite M
Anaheim, CA 92807
(888) 545-8618
http://softexpressions.com
(Quilting supplies, fabric paints, transfer supplies, computer-related items, threads)

The Textile Directory
E-mail: orders@textiledirectory.com
Website: www.thetextiledirectory.com

British directory of embroiderers' resources.

Wet Paint Inc.
1684 Grand Avenue
St. Paul, MN 55105
(651) 698-6431
www.wetpaintart.com
(Art supplies, Pebeo paints)

The Woolery
PO Box 468
Murfreesboro, NC 27855
(800) 441-9665
www.woolery.com
(Feltmaking supplies)

Rainbow Silks
6 Wheelers Yard, High Street
Great Missenden, Bucks
HP16 0AL
England
www.rainbowsilks.co.uk/
(Kato liquid clay, ExtravOrganza, Softsculpt)

Stewart Gill
www.stewartgill.com
U.K. supplier with worldwide shipping; Byzantia paints, Glitterati fusible film, Fresco flakes.

Further Reading

FiberArts magazine

Campbell-Harding, Valerie and Maggie Grey, *Stitch, Dissolve, Distort*, Interweave Press, 2007

Brackmann, Holly, *The Surface Designer's Handbook*, Interweave Press, 2006

Beal, Margaret, *Fusing Fabric: Creative Cutting, Bonding and Mark-making with the Soldering Iron*, Batsford, 2005

Beaney, Jan and Jean Littlejohn, *A Tale of Two Stitches*, Gemini Press Ltd, 2003 (www.doubletrouble-ent.com)

Beaney, Jan and Jean Littlejohn, *Stitch Magic: Ideas and Interpretation*, Batsford, 2005

Campbell Harding, Valerie and Maggie Grey, *Layers of Stitch: Contemporary Machine Embroidery*, Batsford, 2004

Grey, Maggie and Jane Wild, *Paper, Metal and Stitch*, Batsford, 2004

Grey, Maggie, *Raising the Surface with Machine Embroidery*, Batsford, 2006

Hedley, Gwen, *Surfaces for Stitch: Plastics, Films and Fabrics*, Batsford, 2004

Detail of *Fish Bones* bag. Paper clay on cocoon strippings (see page 3 for the complete bag).

Index